FINDING HEAVEN ON EARTH:

FINDING HEAVEN ON EARTH:

The Journey of No Ordinary Preacher

ROBERT W. BOSTON

Finding Heaven on Earth:
The Journey of No Ordinary Preacher
By Robert W. Boston

Published by Boston Books
Charleston, SC

Printed in The United States of America

Designed by Paul Rossmann

Library of Congress Cataloging-In-Publication Data

Boston, Robert W.
Finding Heaven on Earth:
The Journey of No Ordinary Preacher
ISBN 979-8-9856217-0-9

FOREWORD

My father spent the last several years of his life writing these memoirs. He would go to Mepkin Abbey for a silent retreat every year to write. He carried the handwritten manuscript everywhere he went so he could work on it. One time at my brother Richard's house the dog got a hold of it and tore up the first twenty pages. We decided it was time to type it up. Mitch Carnell, his dear friend, who finally lit the fire under my father and convinced him to record his life on paper, said these pages probably needed editing anyway, and so that is how the dog became one of the editors. After this we began to piece the stories together, and I started typing. It took me a while—it was hard and bittersweet to read, and with many tears I typed his words.

Our process went a little like this: I printed out a section and gave it to him to proof. I made corrections. I told him it still didn't feel complete. He had left out stories of his grandchildren, children, and other significant events. We remembered these together, and so he began to add some stories.

What he had envisioned as a memoir of his professional life turned into something much more personal. We have included memories from his brother and sister, children, grandchildren, and my mom. In the last year of his life, he had a hard time keeping thoughts in his head and he couldn't seem to write, so together we wrote the chapter "Living in the Village" and finished it just a week before the end of his life with us.

At times throughout this process, I couldn't bring my-self to complete it—I didn't want the story to end. With the help of the family (his children and grandchildren), I finished writing the last two chapters "Living on Hospice" and "Studying Heaven," about becoming a mystic.

These are a compilation of our memories with Dad. We want this to be a record of his incredible life for us and generations to come.

—Robin Lynn Boston

PREFACE

The Sunday after Pa left this life for the new, I sat down with his sermons, handwritten on lined paper, filed in a box under my bed. I had saved them knowing I would long to sit with Pa and his wisdom in the days when I could not call him up or be by his side.

As I immerse myself in Pa's written words, more and more I realize that I must have garnered my gift of writing from my PaPa. I had long wondered where this came from, my passion for words, for weaving together ideas, forging connections between see amingly unlike objects, ideas, emotions with poetry. PaPa had this, too; his gift for words were woven into his lessons as a minister. For years he stood at the pulpit, sat across from families, held children in his lap, and told stories to teach us.

He too had this ability to weave together ideas, people, places and to make deep connections between seemingly unlike things, revealing to all those who listened the beauty in this complex life, the beauty in the unknown. As I read the sermons he left behind, this beautiful memoir he recorded for us, it is evident that life is not simple, love is not simple, but, oh, how beautiful.

I am so grateful to my grandfather who had the courage, the perseverance, and the passion to write down his life story. May it stand to be a reminder of his teachings, of his love, of the idea that this life is only a beginning. That this beautiful life is only one of many, that our time here is ephemeral and meant to be cherished now.

—Rosalyn Cowart Greene

PROLOGUE

With this book I am fulfilling a promise that I made some time ago to my oldest granddaughter, Rosalyn Cowart Greene, that I would write down the stories of our family life as they have unfolded over the past seventy-eight years. [By the time Bob "finished," it was eighty-seven years.] Through these years I have shared bits and pieces of our journey, but they have always been open-ended, the conclusion left to those listening.

Rosalyn's wedding 3-23-13

I think what Rosalyn would like to know is how this generation of Bostons came from Kansas City, Missouri to the town of Darlington,

Birthday celebration with family ca. 1998

South Carolina, then back to Kansas City, where her mother was born, then on to Monterey, California, and eventually back south, settling for the past forty-plus years in Hanahan, a small suburb of Charleston, South Carolina.

Since most of these moves were initiated for professional reasons and perhaps by some unknown psychological motivation, I suppose I am the one who needs to connect the dots and write down the events and stories that brought us to where we are today.

These are some good stories—some exciting, some sad, others loving, frightening, peaceful, hard to believe, many of them heartfelt. Reminiscing, they all seem to have played a part in who we are and where we are today. Through the years we have remained a close, loving, and supportive family. Every holiday and birthday the family comes together. If a member is not around the same table there will be phone calls from the ones not present. As our children have grown up, moved into their own homes, and had children of their own, they and their spouses have become our best friends. We play together, work together, and celebrate together.

There is another source of encouragement in the writing of my story. I have an old acquaintance who has become a close friend. His name is Mitch Carnell, and he himself is a celebrated and accomplished writer. Mitch and I, along with Rose, graduated from Furman together. Recently, we have shared a lot of stories, including our views about religion, politics, and life in general. When I told Mitch I was thinking about writing my life story, he said, "Great." But that was not the end of it. He brought me a copy of his own life story along with a half- dozen books on how to write a memoir. He has been asking me for a year now, "Have you started your book yet?"

Fulfilling my promise to my granddaughter, who wrote a beautiful poem for my seventy-fifth birthday and promised me she would write a eulogy for my memorial service, my first task was to find a peaceful and quiet place. As I write this prologue, I am sitting in a chair behind a cabin at Mepkin Abbey, a Trappist monastery overlooking age-old oak trees with moss hanging below, bordered by blooming azaleas. In the morning, I will start Chapter 1: "In the beginning."

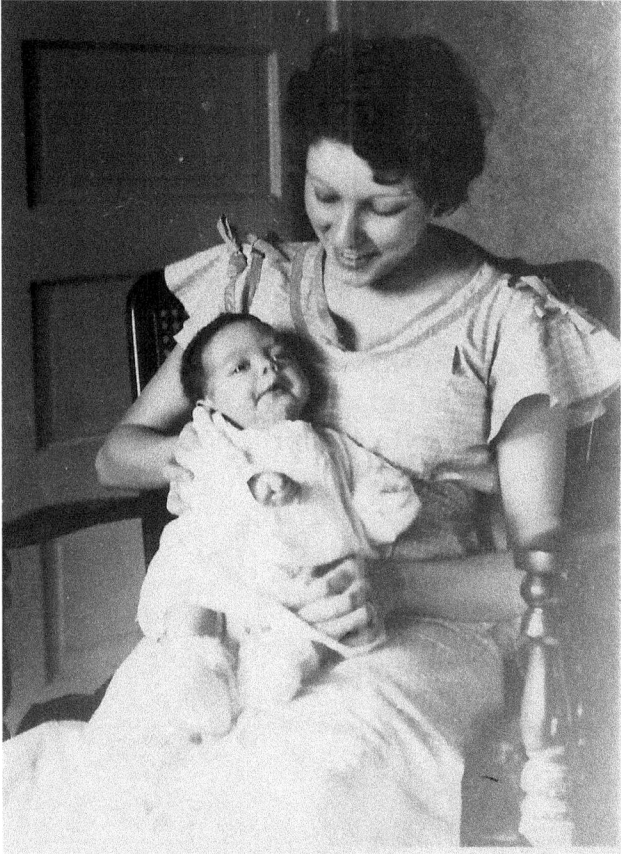

My mother, age 20, holding me at 6 weeks old.

CHAPTER ONE

IN THE BEGINNING

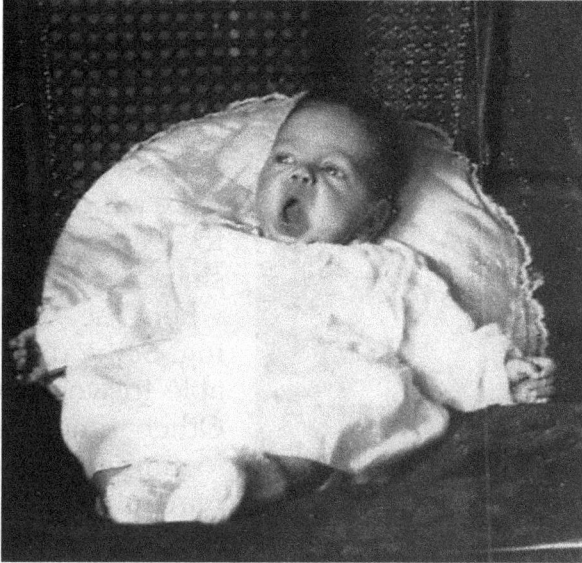

1933, 2 months old

I was born in Kansas City, Missouri in 1933 and there I spent my first six years. I was told later in life that the early 1930s were rough years in Kansas City, especially for young couples getting started in life. The whole country was in a Depression when Mom and Dad were married in 1931. Both were eighteen and had just finished high school. I was born two years later. Mother told me that during the first eight years of their marriage they moved twenty times for such reasons as finding a bigger apartment or one with better furniture, or one that had a refrigerator instead of an icebox. In some cases, they moved because they could not pay the rent.

These were hard times, but I was never aware of it. Dad often worked two jobs at a time and moved from one job

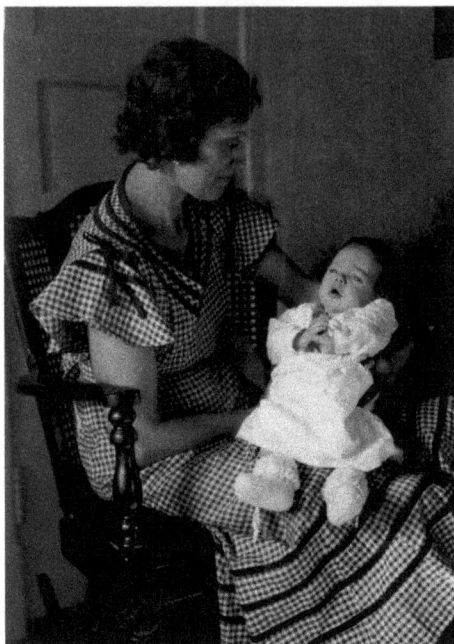

Paternal grandmother Bertha "Nana" 1933 (her 1st grandchild)

1935, Elmo, Peggy, Bobby

to another, I suspect for better conditions or pay. Mother was also working, but after I was born Dad insisted on Mother staying home to take care of me. Some of my first memories were window watching for Dad to come home, since we never knew when he was coming. Some days he was able to work overtime. Other times he went looking for other jobs. I remember hoping that the next car that turned the corner would be his. I was told that I often fell asleep counting cars.

I was proud of my dad. He was bigger and taller than all the other men I had seen. Mom said he was handsome, too. I remember him telling funny stories and he was always bringing some little something home for me. Mom told me that when I was really little, before I could walk or sit up straight, he took me with him on the city streetcar when he was not working, just to show me off. One night he was late coming home while

1935, Mom and me

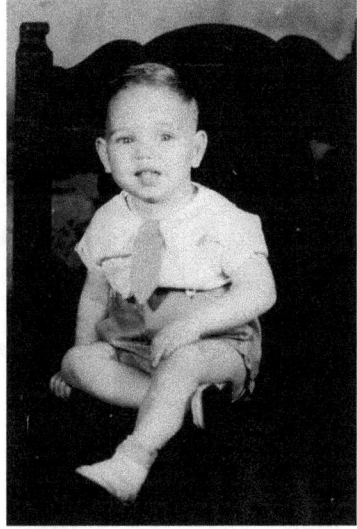

1936

I was with him. Mother went to the local pool hall and found me sitting in one of those "high chairs" that pool halls have, tied to the chair with a diaper, watching Dad shoot pool. My dad, as I learned late, was a gentle, kind, and loving father.

Back to those first six years in Kansas City. When I was five years old, Dad's uncle offered him a job selling life insurance in Nashville, Tennessee. He accepted the opportunity since jobs were becoming more difficult to find in Kansas City. We moved to a suburb of Nashville, a little town called Old Hickory. The family lived there for only a year, and then we moved back to Kansas City because World War II had

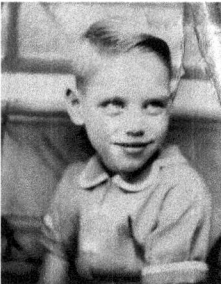

started, and no one was buying insurance. There are two events that I remember during this year in Tennessee. The first was getting my first dog, a German Shepherd. Since I had not started school, he was my only friend. I don't remember where we got him or what we did with him when we moved. I do remember trying to talk Mom and Dad into letting him

1938

1939

go back to Kansas City with us. I've got a picture of him sitting with me on the front step of our house.

The second event happened in a doctor's office. My brother Ronnie was born while we lived in Old Hickory. When he was a week or so old Mom and Dad took him to see the pediatrician. I went with them and while we were sitting in the waiting room, I heard a baby scream. Since I knew that Ronnie was the only baby there, I began to cry, too. When I asked what they were doing to him, Dad told me, I suspect not to get too graphic, that it was something the doctor does to keep little boys from getting infected and a doctor did it to me when I was born, and I screamed, too. I can to this day see that waiting room— black metal chairs covered with maroon cushions.

We went back to Kansas City, but not for long. Dad saw a job opportunity advertised in the *Kansas City Star*. It was with the Hallmark Cards, Inc. and required a move to South Carolina. The job offered a new company car, a trailer filled with greeting cards and stands, and a good salary for that day and time. The job consisted of setting up stands of Hallmark cards in department stores and drugstores throughout South Carolina. The family could live anywhere but preferably in the center of the state. The assignment was for one year.

1941

Despite the disapproval and disappointment of my grand-parents on both sides of the family and Mother's reluctance, the decision was made to move. Sometime during that summer of 1939, Elmo and Peggy Boston, along with their two boys (I was six and Ronnie was two), left Kansas City in a brand-new 1939 Plymouth sedan, pulling a Silver Stream trailer filled with stands and greeting cards, along with all their worldly possessions. My dad had at one time remarked to my mother that he would like to see his boys raised in a small town away from the perils of big-city living. He was about to get his wish.

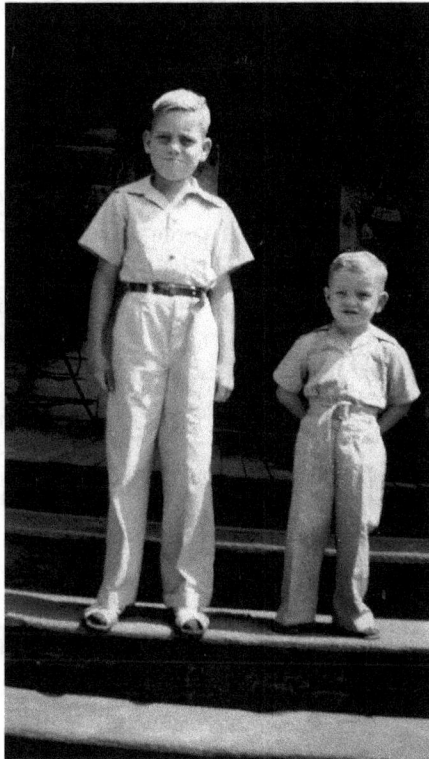

1942, Bobby (9), Ronnie (3)

CHAPTER TWO

EARLY YEARS IN DARLINGTON

1944, Christmas. Me Ronnie and Joy

We settled in Darlington, South Carolina, a small town of six thousand people, supported mostly by agriculture, a cotton mill, and a Dixie-Cup factory. Dad found a small two-bedroom apartment in the home of a retired schoolteacher, Mrs. Pearl Shepard. It was an old Darlington home, well-kept and with a big porch around the front of the house, with green rocking chairs and a jog-

1943, Peggy's Tribe

gling board. Behind the house was a large wooded area where I played cowboys and Indians. Some of my heroes were Sgt. York of World War I, and actors John Wayne, Bob Steele, and Gene Autry. On Saturday mornings, I got to see them at the local theater. On the other side of the woods was a railroad track which was the dividing line between where the white people and black people lived. There were a lot of kids in the neighborhood, but it appeared that all were a year or two older than me. There were times when they invited me to play with them, though they often let me know I was too young to do what they were going to do. I remember sitting on our front porch watching them go by and wishing I could go with them. I mostly played alone.

It was here that I got my first real job, mowing the front lawn for Mrs. Shepard. I remember one rule, "Don't leave any ribbons." I didn't know what ribbons were. I had never lived in a place that had a green-grass lawn. My second job was carrying coal in what was called a scuttle up to the third floor of an elderly lady's big house next door. My third job was tying tobacco leaves together at the tobacco warehouse, about four blocks away.

My dad was gone during the week, traveling throughout the state selling Hallmark cards. Mom was busy keeping house and taking care of Ronnie. Dad often said when he left home that I would have to be the man of the house while he was gone. Those words gave me a sense of pride but also became an injunction that I lived with my entire life. I'm not sure whether to call this a curse or a blessing; maybe it is both.

My sister Joy was born

1943, Bobby and Joy in the cornfield.

about a year after we moved to Darlington. I remember vividly the morning she was born. It was in the front room of our apartment, overlooking the front porch. I had heard Mom and Dad talking about calling the doctor. The next thing I knew, Dr. Edwards came and was with mother in the front bedroom with the door shut. Suddenly I heard a loud groan coming from the bedroom. Frightened, I asked Dad, "What's the doctor doing to my mother?" In a few moments I heard a baby screaming. It was like that time in Old Hickory when Ronnie was circumcised. Everything turned out good and I got to hold my baby sister.

While we were living at Mrs. Shepard's house I was convicted for my first and last major crime. I was nine years old. It happened this way: A new kid (I cannot remember his name, so I will just call him Johnny) moved into our neighborhood on Broad Street, about two blocks from our house. He looked about my age. He was walking down the sidewalk in front of our house. I was sitting on our front steps. He came over and told me that he was new in the neighborhood and asked me to come to his house to play. I asked Mom if I could go and she said yes, since she could see his house from ours. Johnny's mother was not at home. He said she'd gone to the store and would be back soon. For a time we swung on a tire swing. Then Johnny suggested that we walk to the town square, about ten blocks away.

The business section of Darlington is on the square, surrounded by a large red-brick courthouse, banks, and offices. There were two dime stores on the square, McClellan and Rose's. Johnny suggested that we walk through the dime stores. I was feeling like I had aged a bit, being away from home, making my own decisions as to where to go. Mother would never have allowed me to go this far away from home without a parent. I had reasoned as much as a nine-year-old could, that I would just be gone less than an hour and if she asked where I had been, I would tell her, "playing in Johnny's backyard." Having a ready-made excuse seemed important.

After we walked through the dime store and were out on the street, Johnny took several items out of his pocket, like a key chain, a gold necklace, a bracelet, and several other trinkets. I asked him where he got the money to pay for these things. He told me he didn't and that it was easy. When the clerk was busy helping someone else, he picked up what he wanted and put it in his pocket.

Wow! I thought, this is big-boy stuff.

Not wanting to feel like a mother's little boy, I did the same thing in the second dime store. When I got home about an hour later, I noticed that Dad's car was in the driveway. That was unusual. He seldom came home in the middle of the afternoon. I did not worry about Mom; I could usually get by her. But Dad, if anything was wrong or out of place, he would see it. In order to protect myself I went around to the back door. There was a coal pile near our back steps. I stopped there and took my loot and placed it carefully under chunks of coal. Then I walked in the house.

Dad was reading the morning paper. Mother confronted me with a sharp, pointed question, "Where have you been?" I told her I had been playing in Johnny's backyard. Dad did not look up from his paper, which seemed unusual. After a few moments, which seemed like hours, Dad asked me a question in a rather calm voice, "What did you put under the coal pile when you came home?" I had to think up an answer quick. I told him I was just straightening up the coal. Then he said, "I think I saw something shiny under the coal. Let's go see what's there." Dad in his calm way picked up the trinkets and carried them inside the house. He then picked up the telephone and said he needed to call the police. Mother tried to talk him out of it. I began to cry and begged him to whip me instead.

Ten minutes later a police car pulled in front of our house. The police chief, Peele Privette, dressed in his uniform, and Detective Tart, who wore a coat and tie, came into the house. Dad took them into the living room with me and shut the door. I felt ashamed, hurt, and scared. For about thirty minutes they asked me questions and described life in a reform school for boys, the penalty for robbing two stores. I was very frightened. My sentence was to stay at home under the guidance of my parents. They explained that if I was caught stealing again I would be sent to reform school. Dad never said another word.

I found out years later that I had been set up. The clerk in the dime store knew Mom and Dad. When she saw me out with this new boy in town, who previously had been caught stealing, she called my parents. I had been caught before I was guilty! This was "tough love," before the term existed. Maybe this is the reason my dad wanted to raise his boys in a small town.

CHAPTER THREE

LIFE ON SPRING STREET

1944, Cub Scouts

Becuase Dad's job with Hallmark was going well, he and Mother decided to look for a house they could buy instead of continuing to rent. They found a three-bedroom house on the other side of Darlington. It was located on Spring Street, where many of Darlington's prominent families lived; our house was the smallest in the community. People often had to ask twice what our last name was because they had never heard of a family named Boston. I told people—as I have many times since—that it was just like the city in Massachusetts. I don't think that went over so well in a small southern town that flew the Confederate flag next to the American flag. As you might imagine for a wealthy neighborhood, there were no other kids my age. I was nine years old and continued to play alone except when I was in school. My dear mother solved that problem. She volunteered to start a Cub Scout troop. We had eight to ten boys who came over to our house every Wednesday afternoon. We had a big front yard and a lot of trees in the backyard, a good place for a Cub Scout troop.

I looked forward to Wednesday afternoons. I felt special because we were meeting at my house and my mother was the den mother. It was in this group that I met some buddies who became life-long friends and with whom I have stayed in contact to this day. There was Jimmy Bailey, an avid tennis player in both high school and college and who later was ordained as a Methodist minister. There was Clyde Gardner, always the best dressed among us and whose family had the biggest car. Clyde spent his young childhood on a farm, graduated from Clemson, and became a very successful electrical engineer. Another lifetime friend was Cecil Durant, who dropped out of college to join the Air National Guard and later became a Delta pilot for more than thirty years.

The Boston family was beginning to look like a prosperous southern family—as long as you didn't go inside our house, which was partially furnished with second-hand furnishings. The house was heated by a wood-burning stove that stood in the middle of the dining room. The bedrooms and living rooms were closed off in the winter. Mother joined the Order of the Eastern Star, a group related to the Masons, and became involved in community projects. Dad got a family membership in the Darlington Country Club and played golf on weekends. Caddying became my fourth job. I loved caddying for my dad. He did not tip me like the other men, but the chance to be with him for four to five hours was more important than getting tipped. Dur-

1952, Spring Street, Darlington, SC. Me (2ⁿᵈ from left), friends and my grandmother, Gonga and Joy.

ing my preteen years I spent a lot of time at the club playing golf and swimming in Black Creek. I could walk there from our house—it took about an hour—but I usually caught a ride by sticking out my thumb. I played with Dad's clubs even though they were too big. I made some adjustments and actually got pretty good as a junior player. I played a lot with the golf pro's son. His name was also Bobby. He had some nice-looking clubs cut down to fit a young boy and a golf bag with covers for his woods. Dad's clubs were a mixture of different names that he had bought at the used-furniture store. Some had wooden shafts. I was sort of ashamed of the clubs, but I found out that if I stood far enough away nobody really paid any attention to the kind of clubs one had.

By the time Ronnie went to kindergarten he was doing what all other healthy five-year-olds were doing, mainly being a pest. Joy was still in diapers. When Mother had to be away, I was the one left to watch over them. I was still the man in the family when Dad was away on business. Joy was easy to care for, but Ronnie was in the terrible fives. He tested my patience. One winter night he acted out so much that I locked him in the living room, which had no heat. He cried and screamed. There were double window-pane doors between the dining room and living room, which I locked. I put my face up to one of the glass panes and stuck out my tongue at him. That rascal took his five-year-old fist and busted through the glass; the pieces cut my head just above my left eyebrow. I've still got a scar that is more than eighty years old to prove he did it. Mother got on both of us for fighting but blamed me the most. I think now that nine-year-old boys should not take care of a five-year-old and five-year-old boys should not be made to listen to those who are nine years old.

Dad's brother Ronnie remembers this incident slightly differently in his entry later in this book. He remembers it as his first memory, "and here I surmise is the reason: The living room, in addition to having no heat, was also very dark, and Bobby was 'booing' at me like a 'boogie man' and sticking his tongue out with his face against a glass pane at about my height.... Bobby has ... [the] scar above his left eyebrow. Well, I also have proof of that event, by an eighty-one-year-old scar on the inside of my left forearm."]

The Boston family seemed to be settled and doing well in their new home, at least by outward appearances. But it would not last long. The year was 1943. The war in Europe and the Pacific was escalating. Dad and Mom thought that Dad might not be drafted since he had three small children, but a draft notice arrived in the mail. Two days later he got on a Greyhound bus bound for Fort Jackson near Columbia, South Carolina, to be inducted into the U.S. Army.

I remember wondering whether I would I ever see my daddy again. At night I cried myself to sleep. And when I woke in the morning I cried some more. I did not cry in front of Mom, Ronnie, and Sis because I remember my Dad saying that when he was away I had to be the man of the house. I now think that no young boy—or girl, for that matter—should be given that kind of responsibility. It has shaped my life for better and for worse to this very day.

To the surprise and delight of the whole family, about a

week after Dad left for Fort Jackson an army bus pulled up in front of our house and he got off. He told us that he did not have to go into the army because he was over thirty years old and had three children. He had a deferment; I didn't know what that word meant, but I was glad I did not have to be the man of the house any longer. Or so I thought.

For a time, our family seemed to get back to where we were supposed to be—Mom was at home being the den mother, Dad went back to work, Ronnie was an aggravating five-year-old, Sis was a sometimes cute and sometimes terrible three-year-old, and I was slowly becoming the man I was supposed to be. I was about to enter the fourth grade at St. John's grammar school.

1952, Peggy, Gonga (Peggy's Mom, my Grandmother), Bobby, Elmo, Joy & Ronnie

CHAPTER FOUR

ELEMENTARY SCHOOL DAYS

Ms. Jones was my fourth-grade teacher. I was already in love with her because she had been my second-grade teacher, too. I liked her in the second grade and loved her in the fourth grade. I remember believing that I was her favorite student even though I knew I was by far not the smartest student.

For the most part I enjoyed my grammar-school days. While I wasn't the smartest, I made up by trying to be the most helpful. Some of my fondest memories were washing the blackboard after school with a rag and a bucket of water, cleaning the fishbowl in the little creek behind the school and running errands for the teacher. I remember how important I thought I was when the teacher asked me to take something to the office. I figured she must have trusted me more than the others to go somewhere by myself. I guess it was more like being "the man of the house."

One of my most memorable moments in elementary school was finding ways to avoid the bullies who teased me before, during, and after school. The bullies were easy to recognize because they usually traveled in threes. They wandered around the school grounds at recess looking for shy city boys like me. Their way of bullying was to catch you by the arm and try to pound a "frog" on your arm with their fists. Often, they took turns to see who would deliver the biggest frog. The more their victim resisted or cried the more they beat up on him. To avoid them on the playground I stood close to a teacher. If a teacher was not present, I went to the rest room and sat on the toilet.

One of the meanest bullies was a student I'll call Jack. He was a short, wiry boy, with sandy, reddish hair and freckles all over his face, arms, and legs. One day my fear of bullies turned to exuberant confidence. It came about this way: It was Saturday afternoon and I took my brother Ronnie to the movies. I must've been around eleven years old and in the sixth grade, Ronnie was six years old and

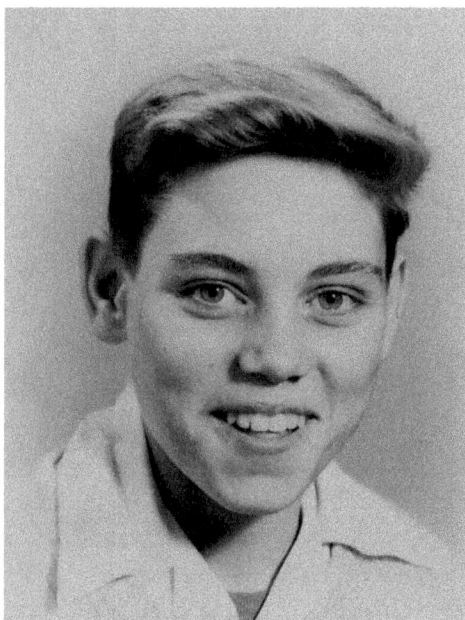

Me at age 13, 1946

wanted to sit in the front row. Just before the movie was to begin, I noticed out of the corner of my eye that Jack and a couple of other bullies were sitting directly behind us. Fear took a grip on me and I began to slouch in my seat. As the movie began, in his excitement Ronnie stood up in his seat. Then I heard a familiar but terrifying voice, "Boy, you better sit your little ass down." I immediately pulled my brother down. But a few minutes later Ronnie got excited again and stood up. At which time, Jack reached across the seat and popped Ronnie beside the head. Never before and never since have I felt so much adrenaline rise up in my body. It was like a monster rose up out of my insides ready for battle. Never before and never since have I felt such strength and confidence.

I jumped over those front row seats, grabbed Jack by his shirt, ripped off every button, and dragged him out of his seat. I slammed him down on the aisle of the theater. Within seconds, it seemed, the manager and ticket-taker pulled

Me at age 14, 1947

me off Jack and led us both to the sidewalk in front of the theater, followed by my brother. Then and there I continued my attack on Jack. I was pulled away by the manager and told that if we didn't take our fight somewhere else, he would call the police. Jack suggested that we go to the alley behind the Belk's store. I was eager and ready. Apparently, the monster in me had not left and I again pulverized his face and body in the back alley across from the city jail until he said, "Enough! I've had enough." It would have been good if we had shaken hands, but the monster in me hit him again. I remember saying, "This is for my brother."

This was not the end of this affair. I could not wait until school started on Monday morning. I got to school early and walked around looking for other bullies. I continued looking for them at recess but there were none to be found. Word had gotten around that somehow Bobby Boston had beaten up Jack Smith.

In seventh grade I started dating—or at least spending time with girls. I considered Margaret Cromer my first real girlfriend, though I never admitted that to anyone, even her. Margaret lived out in the country, down a dirt road about two miles from Darlington. We were both in the seventh grade. She lived with her mother, dad, and big brother. On occasions my mom and dad would visit the Cromers and I would go along. Margaret was not just a country girl. She was smart, kind, attractive, sweet, and everything I would have hoped for in a girlfriend.

I remember my first visit to her home, when I hoped to become more than just a friend of the family. I got up the nerve to ride my bicycle down that dirt road to see Margaret. When I got there, I was exhausted, sweaty, and dirty. Margaret and her mom and dad were just getting ready to eat lunch. They invited me to join them for ham sandwiches, pickles, potato chips, and sweet tea, a kind of lunch I enjoy to this day. But back to my embarrassing moment that took the place of my telling Margaret I liked her more than just as a friend. As I began to take the first bite of my sandwich, Mr. Cromer asked if I would like to add some salt. I recall thinking that if he asked, I should say yes. Instead of passing a salt shaker he passed the bowl of salt. I must've wondered how I would get the salt from the bowl to my sandwich. But I saw Mr. Cromer pick up salt with two fingers and he rubbed them together. So I did the same, trying to give the impression that I did this all the time.

My problem began when I picked up too much salt and instead of rubbing my fingers, I dropped a big pile right in the middle of my sandwich—to the obvious astonishment of everyone at the table. Mr. Cromer remarked, "I think you might have put too much salt on your sandwich. Let me get you another sandwich." To keep myself from feeling embarrassed I said, "Oh, no. I like a lot of salt on my sandwiches." When I started gasping and coughing, Mr. Cromer took me to the bathroom. My opportunity to tell Margaret that I liked her was over. As soon as I could I thanked them for the lunch, got on my bike, and rode home as fast as I could.

I didn't return to Margaret's house until we were in high school and she invited some friends to a party. I recall thinking in the back of my mind that maybe she had forgotten the salt episode and we could start a friendship. I discovered that she had become the girlfriend of Tommy Stokes, known as the best-looking boy, the best athlete in the school, and the son of the Darlington County sheriff. My search for a true girlfriend had to wait, and all because I didn't know how to put salt on my sandwich.

1949, AGE 16

CHAPTER FIVE

High School Days—Girls

In the 1940s high school began in the eighth grade. I recall feelings of fear and intimidation. I suspect part of this anxiety was due to leaving seventh grade and feeling older, wiser, bigger, and more experienced than those in the lower grades; and I was no longer afraid of the bullies. But now I was about to enter high school where I would be one of the younger students—not so wise, big, or experienced. Added to this fear and uncertainty were the stories that had been passed down through the grammar-school grades of the horrible initiations that all freshmen had to face. The alternative, I figured, was to quit school. I hoped that most of these stories were exaggerated. Actually, there was more of a school spirit and a kind of acceptance than I had expected, especially at high school ball games where freshmen were appreciated as much as upperclassmen. There was a sense of pride in being called a St. John's Blue Devil. To my surprise and delight there were no bullies to deal with.

My high-school days came with three priorities: find a special girlfriend, play sports, and make passing grades, in that precise order. Thinking, looking, maneuvering, and speculating about girls took place even when I was playing sports or studying. I remember thinking it would be good to have a steady girlfriend to walk with to school. In addition, if I had a steady girlfriend I would not have to worry about my fears of calling a girl for a date. I was so bashful that I called my best friend, Jimmy Bailey, who could talk to anybody on any subject, and asked him to call the girl I was interested in. I wanted him to ask her,

"If Bobby Boston were to call to ask you to go to such and such a party would you go?" If she said yes, I called her. I know that sounds absurd, but it's true and that made finding the right girl difficult. For the most part I found myself content for most of my freshman year in high school to go to ballgames, banquets, the Darlington Teenage Club, and special parties with a boyfriend or a group of boys.

By the spring of my freshman year, those plans began to change. My first date with a girl was in the eighth grade, at the Sweetheart Banquet at the First Baptist Church. Even though my mother and dad where members of the Darlington Presbyterian Church I had joined the Baptist church because that was where most of the young people attended. Being freshly baptized I was eligible to attend the banquet. My dilemma was who to take. Since I was new in the church and had not been attending the youth groups, I did not know any of the girls there.

My mother made a suggestion. She had a friend from the Order of the Eastern Star who had a daughter about my age. Her name was Judy Banks and she lived only about two blocks from us. I remembered seeing her at school. She was attractive, had long blonde hair, blue eyes, and was about as tall as I was, but I had never met her. My next problem was figuring out how to ask her. I had always been—and still am—shy and insecure around girls. After hours of rehearsing what I would say if she said yes or if she said no, I finally called. I don't remember how I asked, but I remember what she said— "Yes, I would like to go." So we went, and that is a story never to be forgotten.

Transportation in that day was a problem. I was not old enough to drive and normally in this situation my mother or dad would be the chauffeur to any event. My problem was that my dad only had a pickup truck and he was seldom home in the evening. I tried to think of some other parents we could ride with but could not come up with any. But then Mother and I talked to Dad and he agreed to take us. I remember asking him to make sure the truck was clean. The banquet was to begin at 6:30 p.m. The dress was formal—coat, tie, and evening dress. Mother said it was customary to give your girlfriend a corsage so she picked out a yellow one. I had told Judy I would pick her up at 6:15. I told my dad 6 o'clock so he would not be late.

At 6 o'clock sharp I stood on our front porch, nervous and anxious, hair oiled back, with tie, blue coat, and white pants, holding a yellow corsage. With each minute, I grew more nervous, until 6:15 came. Then I panicked, almost cried, and imagined how terrible that would be on my very first date.

Mother again came to the rescue. She told me that if I started walking, I would be at Judy's house in five minutes and by that time my dad would probably be there to take us. I started walking. I got to Judy's house at 6:20. She opened the door and stood there, her blond hair draped over her shoulder. She had on a floor-length, light-green evening dress with a pearl necklace. She looked beautiful. I was out of breath, having walked fast for two blocks and didn't know what to say. She also did not say a word. After what seemed like an evening gone by, I handed her the corsage. She smiled, and said she would be right back. I waited on her porch anxiously looking for Dad. When he didn't show, I thought about making an excuse for him and hoped her mother would offer to take us. But I soon found out her dad did not live with them and her mother did not have a car.

After re-pinning Judy's corsage on her dress her mother smiled and said the church was only a few blocks away and Judy was used to walking. Embarrassed, I worried that some of the other young people riding with their parents would see us walking down Main Street. I felt that I couldn't take a chance, so I suggested to Judy that we take a "shortcut," which meant that we would go down the back streets in Darlington, where the "colored folks" had their stores and eating places. But at least we would not be seen by any of our friends going to the banquet. Judy did not object, so that's the way we went.

The banquet went well. The food was good, there was music and dancing, awards given for best dressed both for boys and girls, and the best-looking couple. I thought for a brief moment we might win something. Several older teenagers said how nice we looked. Mrs. Banks (no relation to Judy) said we looked good as a couple. For some reason that I could not figure out, Judy did not talk much at all. In fact, I only remember two phrases the whole evening, "Thank you, that is nice." The evening ended with a song. We walked home the same way we came without a word spoken until we arrived at the front door. Then she said, "Thank you," with a smile. That ended my first date.

Later that year, Eleanor Jane Howle, one of the girls in our crowd, planned a party in her backyard around a campfire. She invited boys and girls who often congregated at school, church, the playground or neighborhood, and at birthday parties. That is what constituted "the crowd"— young people with similar interests, backgrounds, family trees, living arrangements, customs, race, values, and finances. Those in our crowd came mostly from average middle-class families. We were classified as "good" kids from "good" families.

Going to a teenage party without parental supervision was something new for me and I think for most of the young people there. After refreshments—roasted hot dogs, marshmallows, chips, and Cokes—we all ended up sitting in a circle. Someone suggested that we play "Spin the Bottle." I could not imagine how spinning a bottle could be any fun. I soon learned differently.

The rules were that the person whose first name was closest to the letter "A" would be the first to spin the bottle in the middle of the circle. The object of the game was that whoever the bottle pointed toward, the spinner of the bottle would take him or her over behind the large oak tree and be the kisser. Then the kissee went to the center of the circle and spun the bottle and repeated the same scene on and on. I remember that knots were tying up in my stomach. No one could see how nervous I was because the only light was the flickering of the fire. I remember that for the first time in my life and probably the last time I called myself Robert. I was afraid that "Bobby" would be the closest to the letter A.

Up to this time in my life I had never kissed anyone except my mom, dad, and baby sister, along with a couple of grandparents, and that was only on the cheek. I wondered, What would a girl think if I just kissed her on the cheek? That fear was alleviated when I realized that since my name was Robert on this night, I would be the kissee the first time rather than the kisser. Then I could follow suit. As the bottle began to spin my insides spun much faster than the green Coke bottle. Bashful me was silently praying, "Oh, God, please don't let it point to me." God must have answered my prayer for it was a while before I became the kissee. I have tried to remember the girl who picked me for the first time but cannot. I suppose my emotions at that moment overwhelmed any memory capacity. I do remember the kiss. She gently put her hands on my shoulders as if to say, "Don't get too close" and then kissed me with her lips tightly closed. I responded by placing my hands gently on her hips and keeping my lips tightly puckered. That experience inauspiciously began my romantic life, behind an old tree.

That was the first of many such parties over the next couple of years. I don't think I ever missed one. The parties were held in different homes of our crowd. I never had a party at my house because I was afraid my dad would come home after drinking too much and would spoil the party. I do recall that as parties progressed lips became softer, sometimes even parted, bodies stood closer, and kisses lasted longer. I remember thinking, "I wish people would call me Bob instead of Bobby." Bob sounded so much more grown-up and romantic. I had dropped the name Robert.

One party stood out more than the rest, a get-together at Carolyn Stone's house. Carolyn lived in a three-story home with big columns in front. It was located on Cashua Street, one of the main streets that ran through Darlington. We didn't play Spin the Bottle anymore. Someone came up with a new game called "Post Office." The objective was the same, but a little more daring and sophisticated. The rules were that you could purchase a stamp that was either a "one-cent stamp," which entitled you to a hug without a kiss, or a " three-cent stamp," which bought you a hug and a kiss with lips closed, or an "air-mail stamp," which came with a hug and the short kiss with your mouth open, or a "special-delivery stamp" that bought you a hug and a long "wet" kiss! Someone volunteered to start by picking a stamp, then called on someone to honor the value of the stamp. The delivery took place in a closet. I remember the bashful me on the inside telling the confident-looking me on the outside, "What if nobody picks you?"

My fear of rejection disappeared when shortly after the game began Rose Erwin picked me with a special-delivery stamp. Not only did she pick me once, but every time someone picked her, and that was often, she in turn picked me. Rose was one of the most popular and attractive girls in our crowd. I had noticed her ever since we were in the second grade. I had heard that she was one of the smartest girls in school. She was always dressed neatly, had beautiful hair, and good-looking legs. She looked even more glamorous when she took off her glasses before our kiss in the closet. I was curious—and clueless—as to why she picked me over and over again. That helped me shed my bashfulness at parties.

My first "steady girlfriend" was Frances Boykin, who was new in town. Her family had recently moved from Georgetown. I cannot remember when or how I met her. I suspect that due to my shyness she took the initiative. She was a cute girl, with blond hair, and dressed a bit more fashionably than the other girls in our crowd. The stories that she shared about her life before moving to Darlington sounded like something out of a fairy tale.

Frances grew up at Hobcaw Barony, the winter plantation of Bernard Baruch, one of America's most famous and wealthiest statesmen. Her dad was the superintendent at the barony. Baruch was known to have advised several United States presidents and congressmen from a park bench in front of the White House. Frances shared that on numerous occasions she sat on the laps of President Franklin Roosevelt and Winston Churchill, both of whom visited the plantation every winter. She mentioned that she had a boyfriend from Manning, South Carolina, who was a jockey and rode in many races. All of these stories were hard for me, as a boy from a lower-middle-class family, to imagine. My only exposure to such living was in picture books.

At first, I thought she was making all this stuff up until one day her dad asked me if I would like to go to Georgetown with them and meet Bernard Baruch. I remember that day as if it were yesterday. In fact, I remember more about that day than I remember what I did yesterday.

I was awestruck as we drove into Hobcaw Barony in Mr. Boykin's big black Oldsmobile 98. I recall being speechless as the family shared their memories of the past. I remember the drive down the narrow dirt roads, and the gigantic forest as if there were no end. Then there suddenly appeared a large red-brick, four-story mansion, bigger than any house I had ever seen. In the back of the mansion was a six-car garage with an automobile in each bay. Behind the garage was a large horse stable that looked like the big house except it was only one story. To the left of the stable was a large ranch-style house, which had been the Boykins' home before they moved to Darlington. As we parked in the back of the big house, I remember Mr. Boykin saying, "Bobby, you haven't said a word. Are you nervous?" I said, "No, I'm just enjoying the scenery."

As we entered the side door into a big kitchen there stood a large-chested man dressed in what appeared to be a black tuxedo with a bowtie. Mr. and Mrs. Boykin along with Frances greeted him merrily with hugs and kisses. Then Mr. Boykin said, "I want you to meet our new friend, Bobby Boston." As he reached to shake my hand, I said to him what I had been rehearsing in my mind ever since we had left Darlington, "It is a pleasure to meet you, Mr. Baruch." Everyone began to laugh. I wondered what was so funny. Then Frances told me that this was Mr. Baruch's chef, the person who planned all the meals for Mr. Baruch and his friends. The time did arrive, but to me it seemed like hours later, when another man who was tall and lanky, also wearing a tuxedo with a bowtie, came into the kitchen and said to Mr. Boykin, "He is ready to see you now in his library."

As we entered the library, there he stood, Bernard Baruch, tall and even more distinguished than I had imagined. Taller than any man I had ever seen, with gold rimless glasses, dressed casually in a white shirt, red tie, black pants, and a gray vest with a gold chain hanging from one vest pocket to the other. He greeted the Boykins with hugs and kisses, just as the chef had done, then he turned to me and said, "Who do we have here?" After Mrs. Boykin said, "This is Bobby Boston, Frances's new boyfriend." I tried to remember my rehearsed greeting, but I could not. Mr.

Baruch extended his hand to shake mine; with his other hand on my shoulder, he said, "It is a pleasure to meet you, son." I was speechless.

During the course of the brief conversation, Mr. Baruch asked me what I wanted to do when I finished high school. Caught by surprise, I stuttered a bit because that was a question I had yet to ask myself, which would have been a good answer in itself. Instead, after a brief pause, I told him I wanted to be a forester. In retrospect, I wished I had told him something more important, but being a forester was appropriate, since my dad by then was a pulpwood dealer and at the moment I was sitting in a mansion surrounded by a great forest.

CHAPTER SIX

High School Days—Sports

My high school basketball team, 1952. I'm wearing jersey number 12.

Having accomplished my first priority of having a girl-friend, my interests turned to sports. Throughout grammar school I had attempted to play every game that was available, including marbles. I enjoyed the competition and the camaraderie. High-school games were different. I would have to try out and hope to get chosen.

The two sports that I played most consistently before high school were tennis and golf. While both sports were played in the spring, I managed to play on both the tennis and golf teams my freshman year. I think because I moved from one sport to another in season, I never become a particularly good player in either, but I did enjoy the competition. (To this very day I still enjoy a round of golf and a set of tennis and I still end up mostly on the losing side.) When I was in the ninth grade, I gave up tennis and played only golf. I was the fourth player on a four-player team. During my senior year the top three players graduated and I was the only golfer in high school. The school dropped the golf team and I went back to the tennis team. I was again rated the fourth in the four-player team.

In addition to tennis and golf I wanted to play basketball and football with the "big boys." During my freshman year I tried out for basketball and to my surprise I made the team. I didn't make the traveling squad, but I got to practice every day after school and put on my uniform and sit on the bench at home games. Very exciting. I didn't think twice about going out for football my freshman year. A number of players had recently returned from serving in World War II to finish high school. They were big and tough looking. I even stayed out of their way on the school grounds.

I did better in basketball than any of the other sports, and played all four years. The basketball coach was William Cain, who was also the principal of the high school and the tennis coach. Mr. Cain was one of those men who I secretly adopted as a surrogate father. He was my first of many male mentors. For years I stopped by to see him every time I returned to Darlington, which was three to four times a year until he died at eighty-five in 1993. In my last visit with him I told him my secret and discovered that he already knew. He was known for his brilliance in any subject. He was recognized as an excellent tennis player in South Carolina in both doubles and singles and was also a champion bridge player. He was elected to the South Carolina Tennis Hall of Fame. The USTA-South Carolina website says of him, "He was among the state's top ten players for nearly 20 years (1933 to 1950). He won over 100 championships throughout the state during an era of very few tournaments…. The Recreation Department tennis courts in Darlington are named in his honor." He ran the South Carolina Closed Tournament for more than thirty years.

Another reason I liked being on the basketball team was that it provided a good lesson and experience in sex education. Every year during basketball season the team took a trip to Charleston to play Rivers High School and the College of Charleston freshman team. Arrangements were made for our team to stay overnight in the college gym. Mr. Cain always stayed with his brother, who lived in Pinopolis, thirty-five miles away. The games usually ended around 8:30 p.m. and the coach gave us strict instructions to be in our dormitory no later than 9:30. The team on the whole adhered to those instructions. But by 9:40, or as soon as the coach left to go to his brother's, a few of us were enticed by the bright neon lights of downtown Charleston.

At some point during those nightly trips we stumbled upon Market Street, which was considered very racy. Local girls were warned to stay away from the Market because of the number of sailors who congregated there. We discovered that it was the place to be for excitement and thrills between 10 o'clock and midnight. Every evening sailors by the dozens emerged on Market Street, which was lined on both sides with bars and ladies of the night waiting inside to provide the patrons company for the price of a beer.

We had a plan. There were usually three or four of us and we entered one of the dimly lit bars and occupied a booth. Shortly a waitress came by and asked, "What would you boys like for a drink?" Since none of us drank alcohol and we didn't have enough money to buy it if we did, we told the waitress that we were waiting for a friend to join us and we would order when he came. This gave us about five to fifteen minutes to google-eye the girls and the sailors as they fondled each other. When the waitress returned and asked us about our friend, she reminded us, "If you don't drink, you don't stay." So, we told her, "He must've gone to another bar." We then left and repeated this same performance in the next beer joint. All the while we were waiting for the grand finale, which took place at midnight, when the taxicabs lined both sides of Market Street, waiting for a sailor and a girl to exit the bars. As we watched this scene, we wondered, "Where are they going now?" This is when the fantasies of fifteen- and sixteen-year-old boys took over. You just did not see these kinds of goings-on in Darlington County.

My high school football team, 1952. Front row: I'm wearing jersey number 51.

I went out for football my sophomore year but did not get to play in a game except in the last minute when our team was either way ahead or way behind. In my junior year I played linebacker on defense and as a backup to Harry Blackmon, one of the best high-school running backs in South Carolina. Harry broke all of the St. John's High School scoring and running records, was chosen for the All-State team and played in the annual North Carolina-South Carolina Shrine Bowl. Unfortunately, Harry did not go on to college. After finishing the season his senior year, he dropped out of school and joined the navy. I was expected to take Harry's place as quarterback, but there was no comparison. I could not run as fast and I was not a good passer. However, no one else on the team was better so I was picked to be the quarterback. Eugene Baldwin, our fullback, had an outstanding year and was picked to play in the Shrine Bowl. We lost more games in 1952 than we won, but, being the St. John Blue Devils, we never lost our pride.

Our coach was Jimmy Welch, another one of my surrogate fathers. Coach Welch was "a man's man." He also coached baseball, played golf, fished, hunted, and was an expert in all of them. He never had any children of his own, but it was obvious he was proud of the boys he coached, even those who struggled to make the team. He reminded me before I finished high school that I was probably the only athlete in the history of the school who received a letter in five different sports.

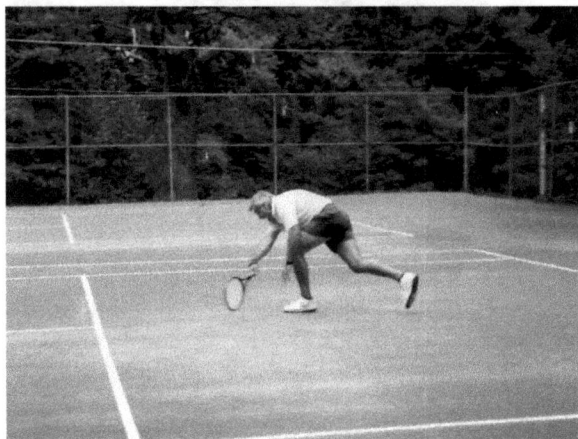
Playing tennis, 1972.

That was my only claim to fame in sports. I tried out for baseball my senior year and found that while I could catch the ball, I couldn't hit it. Coach Welch told me to go back and play tennis.

The most meaningful time in sports for me were those evenings before the games when as a team we left the gym dressed in our pads and uniforms, walked across a swinging bridge boardwalk over a swamp and into the gate at the football stadium, the cheerleaders leading the way, the band playing, and the fans cheering. After a game, the Darlington fans always applauded whether we won or lost. Those were proud moments.

CHAPTER SEVEN

High School Days— Getting an Education

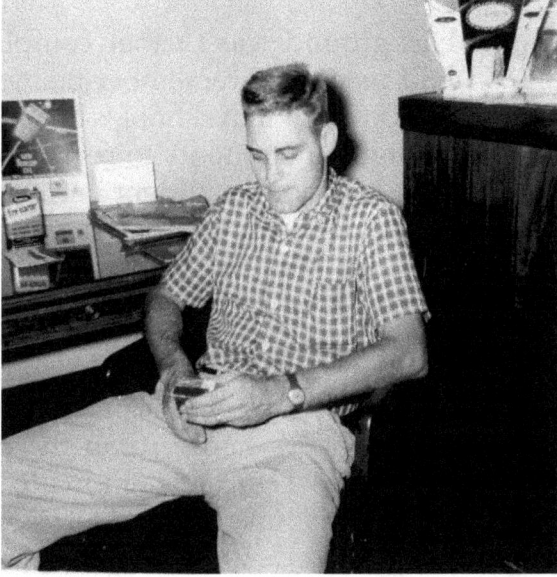

1952, Senior

I am sorry to say, academics were way down on my list of priorities, even though I knew that I would have to make good-enough grades to stay in school, play sports, and continue my friendships.

It was in the beginning of my high-school career that I realized getting a good education was going to be a struggle. Education was not a prime interest in our home. Both my mother and dad finished high school but showed very little interest in further education. I cannot remember any books in our home except the ones I brought home from school and an old set of encyclopedias that dad had bought at the used-furniture store. I don't remember the encyclopedia ever being opened or much interest in my schoolbooks. Mother, being a Christian Scientist, though in Darlington she attended the Presbyterian church, did have a set of religious books which she read every day to herself.

My educational background was further complicated by the difficulties I had reading. I remember being petrified in both grammar school and high school when the teacher began calling on individual students to read a portion of a story. I tried to hide behind the student in front of me so the teacher would not see me and call on me to read. This usually worked. I remember one time when she did call on me, I started coughing, and that worked, too.

I discovered early that my deficiency in reading had a detrimental effect on all my other subjects. I also realized that I was going to have to work harder than the other students to get passing grades. I learned later in life that I had a learning disability that is now called ADHD, Attention Deficit Hyperactivity Disorder. On all my report cards, even in grammar school, my teachers wrote, "Capable of doing better." I worked hard, but still found some success. To my delight and surprise, I excelled in math and Spanish. I did okay in history and social studies, but struggled in English, especially the reading and writing part.

To my surprise I was chosen to be in the National Honor Society when I was in the eleventh grade. However, I was never inducted because Miss Jacquelyn Douglas, the faculty adviser to the society, had my name taken off the list because I told a "nasty" joke in a school play performed before the entire student body. I remember the joke clearly. Jake Patterson and I were doing a skit in the play. We decided to change the joke to one we thought would be funnier. It went something like this: Jake said to me, "Did you know that cows know the exact minute when it's time to eat?" I asked, "How do they do that?" "It's their instinct," said Jake, to which I remarked, "My end stinks, too, but I can't tell when it's time to eat."

The students roared with laughter. Mrs. Douglas roared too, but without a smile.

CHAPTER EIGHT

MY BEST FRIENDS

1954, Tree Company Job

I had many good friends throughout my high-school days, which is an advantage of growing up in a small town and going to a small school. I had four best male friends: Jimmy Bailey, Clyde Gardner, Cecil Durant, and Billy Jones.

Of the four, I spent more time with Jimmy than the others. There was so much that we shared in common. Both our fathers had drinking problems and would have been diagnosed as alcoholics. We both grew up, by today's standards, in lower-middle-class conditions. In those early days neither of our parents owned a home or a car and we both had hand-me-down furniture. We both were the oldest children and were considered caretakers in our family. We both enjoyed sports and girls and we were equally competitive in both. Before school we delivered morning newspapers and often met at Liberty Lunch, the only restaurant open at 6 a.m., to share a toast and jelly. During the summer months before our senior year, Jimmy and I managed the city's clay tennis courts. We also made pimento-cheese and egg-salad sandwiches and sold them to the students at recess. Surprisingly, we made good money and even talked about continuing the business after we graduated. But that is where the similarities ended. Jimmy was outgoing, sociable, talkative, and never met a stranger. He was tall, good-looking, and always managed to dress in the latest styles. He was also the best dancer in school.

Once, Jimmy and I thumbed our way to Myrtle Beach to enjoy the sights and sounds. Of course, one of our goals was to find two girls with whom we could walk around and maybe go dancing. In those days, it always seemed that when two girls were walking together, one was far more attractive than the other. Seldom did we find two good-looking girls walking together. You can imagine who ended up with the plain one! I recall insisting on a plan that if we sighted two potential friends, we would decide ahead who would go with whom. Another difference that I admired in Jimmy was his determination and dedication to every goal he set

Jake and me riding the Blue Ridge Parkway

39

College friends

for himself. When he was still a junior in high school Jimmy made the decision to become a Methodist minister. He never wavered from that commitment and served some of the largest Methodist churches in the North Carolina conference and was almost elected bishop of the conference. He had a strong interest in tennis from the time he was a freshman and he played number-one in high school and college. Later he was ranked as one of the best senior tennis players in North Carolina. I have always admired Jimmy's many accomplishments and how far he has come from where he began. Through the years Jimmy and I have stayed in close touch through visits in each other's homes and frequent phone calls. I love him as a brother.

Clyde Gardner was also one of my special friends. I met Clyde while delivering *The State* newspaper. We both worked for Mr. Sansbury, the manager of deliveries. Clyde's family had recently moved from the country to the big city of Darlington, but they did not act like country folks as I imagined country folks to be. The first time I visited their home I had a hard time believing what I was seeing. They lived in the historic district of Darlington in a large, newly renovated, two-story home with a porch that wrapped around the sides. The yard was exquisitely manicured. The inside was equally attractive and in order. The first time I spent the night with Clyde I noticed the elaborate furnishings and how neat and well-kept the home appeared to be. His dad owned a fish store on the other side of town and his mother managed the home and prepared three big meals a day. I still remember those big breakfasts, consisting of eggs, grits, sausage, and buttered toast. To this day I cook toast just as I remember Mrs. Gardner did.

I was somewhat afraid of Clyde's dad. He appeared to be a strict, no-nonsense type of father. I think Clyde was also scared of him at times. He drove a big, black, late-model Pontiac, with all the trimmings. I remember once Clyde and I planned a double date with the hopes of driving the Pontiac. Clyde had recently obtained his driver's license and had assured me he could talk his dad into letting him have the car. It was about fifteen minutes before we were to pick up our dates when his dad finally came home. I was in the other room when I heard his dad give an emphatic no to our hope of having a car for the evening. When Clyde came out, he said, "Don't worry, he'll give in." In a few moments Clyde came back with the keys. I felt like a rich kid, and dreamed of sitting with my date in the back of the 1949 Pontiac.

I did not see Clyde a lot after we stopped delivering papers, probably because he was an exceptional student and did not participate in school sports. He also worked in his father's store. Clyde went on to graduate from Clemson and after a tour in the navy he developed a successful career as an electrical engineer. Clyde and I have stayed in touch through the years by phone and lately by email. We have expressed our differences and worked hard to change each other's political views, Clyde being a right-wing Republican and me a left-wing Democrat, without much success. We've agreed to disagree.

Cecil Durant was my first close friend. It must've been around the sixth grade when we met. Cecil lived one block from our elementary school. We spent a lot of time togeth-

Revisiting Darlington with Cecil and Jimmy

er in those early years, delivering newspapers, being in the Cub Scouts and Boy Scouts and spending time at the Greyhound Bus station where his mother worked. Cecil's father had left home when Cecil was a young child, so he lived with his mom and older sister. I lost touch with Cecil soon after I started high school. He did not participate in sports and somewhere around the eighth or ninth grade his mother moved to Camden, South Carolina, and sent Cecil to Carlisle Military School in Bamberg. It was twenty-five years before I heard from Cecil again. He called my home one evening in the early 1970s from the Charleston International Airport. I asked him what brought him to Charleston. He told me Delta Airlines, where he had been a pilot since he finished college. Rose and I drove to the airport to see him and he took us into the cockpit of his plane, which had stopped for the night. We had a grand reunion.

Billy Jones was my other close friend. I met Billy through his father, who was the minister of the First Baptist Church and another one of my surrogate fathers. Billy and I were in Sunday School together, were baptized together, and were tennis partners on the high-school team. My own family was Presbyterian, but I discovered the Baptist church had a big youth group and that was where most of the young girls attended. That knowledge was worth another baptism. Apart from the youth group, Reverend Jones was a favorite of both young and old. In a day when most Baptists seemed to believe that if you were not a Baptist there was no possibility you could get into heaven. Reverend Jones had a saying that I have never forgotten, "We are first Christians and secondly Baptists." Reverend Jones initiated joint services with other denominations, which was unheard of in the Southern Baptist Church, especially in small towns like Darlington. In some ways Billy seemed like a brother to me since I admired his father and spent many hours in their home. Reverend Jones played a big part in my early years and an even greater part in my young adult life.

My Best Female Friends

I have mentioned earlier my first and brief romance with Frances Boykin, the new girl in town who arrived just in time to help me gain confidence in relating to girls my age. Frances was a sweet girl and we had a good time going to dances, double-dating with Clyde or Cecil, and taking short trips with her mother and dad. But after about two years I began to lose interest in Frances as a girlfriend. I think it was because she seemed more interested in how she looked and dressed than in other school and social activities. She began dying her hair blonde, used what I thought was excessive makeup, and wore expensive designer clothes. I found it hard breaking up because I liked her mother and dad and I knew they liked me.

I had other teenage romances during my high-school days. There was Jackie Privette, my first and only "country girl-friend." She was attractive, intelligent, and fun-loving, not what I expected from a girl who grew up in the country. We had only a few dates, but what I remember most were the dinners with her family. They had a close family and whenever we dated they always invited me to eat.

Then there was Jimsey Oeland, who was a year younger than me. She lived in one of the most exquisite homes in Darlington. Her father was the superintendent of the Darlington Manufacturing Company cotton mill. She had two sisters, Mary and Helen. My friend Jimmy dated Mary and Billy Jones dated Helen. We often went on triple dates together. I took Jimsey to the junior-senior banquet my junior year.

Then there was Sarah Carrigan, to me the most special of all my steady girlfriends. She was a junior when I was a senior. She was elected May Queen, played on the high school basketball and tennis teams, and was the president of the National Honor Society, along with many other honors. She was the youngest of three children in a close-knit family that lived in one of the large historic homes in Darlington. I remember the feeling of pride having her as my date at my final junior-senior prom. I dated Sarah my senior year. The relationship ended when I finished high school.

As I look back at my high school "romances" I notice they all had one thing in common. All the girls lived in close families and well-furnished homes, two things I wanted as a boy but never had. I have questioned myself, "Was it the girls who I liked or their families that I envied?"

When I think about the girls I knew in high school, the one I felt the most comfortable with was Rose Erwin, my kissing partner at our early teenage parties. I suspect I didn't pursue a relationship with Rose because she did not live in a big house with a mother and father, as her father had died when she was two. Her mother, Mrs. Zubie Erwin, raised her alone. Besides, Rose was the girlfriend of the senior-class president Murray Yarborough.

CHAPTER NINE

LEAVING HOME

1952, My father and I at my high school graduation.

My high school days were golden years for me. In those four short years I experienced a lot of joy and pleasure with the friends I made, both male and female, the families that invited me into their homes, my teachers who put up with me talking too much, my coaches who were like fathers to me, my paper-route customers who always had a kind word, and my mother who was always there for me in sickness and in health, in victory and defeat at all ballgames. That's what life was like growing up in a small town like Darlington. The sad and frightening part for me was the realization that my high-school days were coming to an end. My security blanket was being taken away.

My future appeared daunting. Most of my friends were getting ready to go to college, but for me going to college was a far-fetched notion that I had not let myself think about. Even though my grades were good enough and I had talked with friends about which schools I liked, it did not appear in my genes or DNA to go.

In the first place, no one in the Boston family going back three generations had ever gone to college. Secondly, someone in the school guidance program told me that because of my learning disability I probably would not be able to pass an entrance exam. If that was not enough discouragement, I knew there was no extra money in my family, due to my dad's drinking problem. Our only source of income was Mother's job at the Dixie-Cup plant. I seemed destined to find a job at one of the stores or factories near or in Darlington.

Graduation from high school was a very sad time for me. At the end of the ceremony the graduates were all waving their diplomas and talking about where they were going to college. Both my mom and dad were there. Dad had been drinking, but not enough that anyone outside the family would notice. I was proud that I had graduated with my class but in a disappointed sort of way. Like all the other students I had my picture taken with the class and one with Mom and Dad. I pretended I was excited, too. When someone asked, "Where are you going to college," my stock answer was, "I haven't decided yet," as if I had a number of choices. I knew that at the end of this summer most of my classmates would be off to college, but what about me? My mother, who had always been an eternal optimist as well as the spiritual adviser in the family, said to me, "Something good is going to work out for you, just you wait and see." I wasn't so sure.

Mom was right, something good was about to happen. Immediately after graduation I got a job working for Thomas & Howard, a wholesale distribution company, loading food on a truck. I was paid 75 cents an hour, which was not bad pay at that time for a kid just out of high school. I was hoping to get the job permanently.

Sometime about the end of July I received a call from Gene Brown, the co-owner with his brother of the local laundromat and one of my paper-route customers. He asked me directly, "How would you like to go to Wofford College?" I told him, "I can't think of a better place to go but there's no way I could work it out." His next question was, "How soon can you go?" I didn't have an answer. He went on to tell me that he knew about my financial situation at home and he had arranged with Phil Dickens, his former coach and good friend, to give me a scholarship to play football. He said Coach Dickens and Wofford were switching from a single-wing formation to a T-formation and needed a few good quarterbacks. The first practice would begin in two weeks. After getting my breath, I told him with excitement and jubilation, "I can be ready to go in two weeks." I gave a one-week notice to my boss at Thomas & Howard and one day short of two weeks later I was at Wofford College, getting fitted with a helmet, shoulder pads, and practice uniform. What a difference two weeks made! It totally changed my outlook on life.

I got an added bonus when I learned that four of my classmates, Jimmy Bailey, Murray Yarborough, Russell King, and Walt Session, were also going to Wofford. I would not be alone.

Those first two weeks were rough and tough. I thought that since I was one of the quarterbacks, I would be given special treatment, but I discovered that since I was the third-stringer I had to double as a linebacker and a practice dummy for the first and second teams. I didn't complain. The excitement of being in college was worth whatever was handed out. I told Coach Dickens that I would not have any trouble making good grades, but I may have difficulty passing the college entrance exam. He said, "Don't worry about it, I'll take care of it." I knew then I was in college for the next four years.

I enjoyed my first year at Wofford. I didn't party or date very much, juggling my time between football practice and making the grades I needed to stay in school. That was all I could handle.

There were two life-changing events during my year at Wofford. The first was the name change. Until the day I arrived on the Wofford campus, the name that everyone—family, friends, teachers, and acquaintances—called me was Bobby. For some time, I had wanted to be called Bob. To me, the name Bobby sounded like a little boy who had not grown up. The name Bob sounded more mature, suave, manly, and more romantic. I thought to myself, now is a good time to make my name change. So every new person I met on campus—the coaches, students, teachers, and administration—I introduced myself as Bob. On all the papers and forms I wrote down, "Robert W. 'Bob' Boston." Believe it or not, it worked. My only dilemma was to avoid getting into a crowd with the students from Darlington who knew me only as Bobby. That was not too difficult since none of the others were on the football team.

There was one incident when my name change caused me some embarrassment. After I had been at school for a couple of weeks, I wanted to call home to let them know how well everything was going. I called collect and when the operator asked me, "Whom should I tell is calling?" I told her firmly, "Bob Boston." My dad answered the phone and I heard her tell him, "I have a collect call from Mr. Bob Boston. Will you accept the charges?" His reply was immediate and direct, "Operator, I do not know a person named Bob Boston, so I cannot accept the charges," and he hung up. I thought to myself, he must have misunderstood, so I tried again and got the same response. On the third attempt, I said, "Tell him it's Bobby," and he enthusiastically accepted the call.

The other life-changing event happened at the beginning of spring football practice. I woke up one morning and discovered that my right knee had swollen as big as a football. I couldn't stand up. I was taken to the infirmary and told my knee had to be drained. The diagnostic report was good and bad. The bad news was that if I continued to play football, I could have some serious problems. But if I stopped playing ball the knee would probably heal with no further problems. This was not a hard decision. By the time I had my knee operation I had come to the realization that I didn't have the strength or the ability to make a significant contribution to the football program.

About that time, Wofford had a change in coaches. Coach Dickens accepted the head coach position at Indiana. Starting in 1953 Conley Snidow was the new Wofford coach. Coach Snidow told me I could keep my scholarship if I would be willing to work with the team, meeting the needs of the players. After deliberating a month or so I decided to leave Wofford with mixed emotions. On the one hand I loved the school, the campus, my professors, Carlie dormitory, the students, Coach Snidow, and being known as Bob instead of Bobby. On the other hand, Wofford was a liberal-arts school. I had not decided what I wanted to do for the rest of my life, but I knew I didn't want to be a minister, teacher, or businessman, and I didn't feel that I was smart enough to be a doctor. Most students fell into one or the other in these categories. What about me?

CHAPTER TEN

ENGINEERING AT THE UNIVERSITY OF SOUTH CAROLINA

1954, Me and Joy

I made the decision to transfer to the School of Engineering at the University of South Carolina. I'd always been a good student in math and that would help. During the summer before my sophomore year at USC I found a job working for the Asplundh Tree Company. I worked with a crew of eight guys spraying rights-of-way for AT&T. The pay of 75 cents per hour was good and we had the opportunity to travel throughout North and South Carolina, staying in boarding houses. I was excited about going to the university. While I enjoyed Wofford, going to USC was like going from a small town to a big city and, more important, there were girls there.

Fortunately, I did not have to take an entrance exam, as my grades from Wofford were good enough for admission. But I soon found the School of Engineering was hard. Regular students took only fifteen hours, but engineering students had to take eighteen. Most of the courses were in math. Early in the semester I was inducted into the SAE fraternity, which provided an opportunity to meet new people.

1954, Hand standing on the Tree job.

I still found myself being shy at parties and dances. It was hard to go up to a crowd or individual to introduce myself. I waited for someone to introduce himself to me, then I could begin a conversation. I had very few dates while at Carolina, but as in high school I hoped to find a steady girlfriend with whom to go to parties and ballgames. Since I did not have a car, dating was difficult.

In reflection, 1954 was a pivotal year for me. Three dynamic events took place that changed the course of my life for decades to come. Not one came about by my own choosing. Call it fate, providence, coincidence, or predestination; as it turned out, I think God had His hand on it. When the second semester started, I found myself struggling financially to pay for room and tuition. I had enough for the first semester, because I had saved some money from my summer job with the tree company to go along with the money I was making at a part-time job with the South Carolina Highway Department. In talking with one of my roommates, Leon Outlaw, who was from Hartsville,

South Carolina, I found out that he too was struggling financially to stay in school. I am not sure who came up with the idea, but both of us agreed that we would volunteer for the draft, serve two years in the army, and come back and finish school on the G.I. Bill. We set the following Thursday as the day we would go to the army recruiting office and sign up. We chose that Thursday because the next day was the deadline to pay our tuition, which was $200.

I called my mother and told her about my plan and how relieved I felt to no longer be a financial burden for myself and for her. Whenever she wrote me, she always included some money, usually cash, but sometimes a check for $5.00, $10.00, or $20.00. And she added a short note: "Take this money and buy yourself a good meal and remember, 'you can only be poor spiritually.'"

On the following Wednesday, I got a message from the school registrar to call home. Mother or Dad never before had called me at school, so the message sounded urgent. Something must have happened. When I reached Mom, her message was short and direct, like most of her notes: "Bobby, your grandfather just sent me a check for $200 for your tuition. I put it in the mail this morning. You should have it by Friday. Bobo said you could pay him back when you finish school and have a paying job. I got to go now. I'm already late for work. Love you," and she hung up.

She did not give me a chance to reply. After pondering that phone call for only a few minutes, I called Leon and told him I was going to defer joining the army. He told me he was going ahead with his plan. He served two years as a military policeman in Korea and returned in time to be a groomsman in my wedding. I have pondered many times about that phone call and wondered, "What would I be doing today and what would my life be like, and who would be in it?"

The second life-altering event came in the middle of the second semester. It came unexpectedly in the middle of a night when I could not go back to sleep. Ever since I found the opportunity to go to college I wondered, "What am I going to do? What kind of work or profession will I be satisfied with if I finish school?" I liked the image of a civil engineer. I had never met one, but those I saw impressed me with how they dressed—khaki pants, checkered shirts, deerskin boots. I also liked the idea of designing and building roads and bridges. Up to this stage of my education I had not received any kind of guidance, except for the one teacher who told me that the results of my school test indicated that I would not do well in college and should pursue some form of technical education. I began to worry and could not sleep because I had a test in calculus the next morning. I knew I would have to declare a major my junior year, which was only a few months away. Most of my close friends already knew what they were going to do.

I began thinking about the people I admired the most. I thought of the coaches I had in high school. I admired all of them, but I did not think about being a coach. Every coach I knew was outstanding in one or more sports. I wasn't outstanding in any. But on this sleepless night the person who stayed in my mind was Rev. Bill Jones, my minister since I was twelve years old. When I began thinking of what it would be like to be a minister, I had to chuckle at myself. I even thought of what my friends and family would think. My own reaction was one of disbelief.

Over the next several weeks the idea of becoming a minister was invading my mind during the day and part of the night. It was beginning to have an effect on my studies. As much as I tried, I couldn't get the thoughts out of my head. In some ways, the inclination to be a minister was not surprising. I recalled from an early age the satisfaction I experienced when I could help somebody who looked to be in trouble. I attribute this kind of benevolence to Mom and Dad. Before and after my teenage years, Mother often suggested, when I was going to a party, "If you see someone standing alone, go up and make a friend. Or if you notice a girl who is not dancing, go ask her." Both Mom and Dad seemed to be always willing to help friends, neighbors, and even strangers. When Dad was in the timber business during the war, he had German prisoners working for him, and sometimes he brought them home for supper.

I can trace my personal experience with God back to the time when I was very young and lived in Kansas City. I have a vivid memory of having impetigo, big painful boils just above my knees. When I was six years old, in the first grade, Mother said that maybe we should go see a doctor. My response, according to her, was, "God is always with me and he will heal me." She told me years later that she didn't call the doctor because of my childlike faith. The next morning the boils began to dry up and she didn't feel a need to call the doctor. My mother's two favorite Bible verses were, "All things work together for good for those who love God" (Romans 8:28) and the verse "I am with you always" (Matthew 28:20).

My call to the ministry was not dramatic. I did not hear any voices. It was more like an inner urging that happened over time. The nearest thing to a voice calling me took place early in the semester. Our engineering class was simulating a road project on the campus. I was behind a telescope and my classmate was holding a plumb line a block away. I was intrigued with the power of the telescope and began looking at people walking across campus and, briefly, at the girls' dormitory, when all of a sudden, I felt a firm hand on my shoulder. It was my professor with a stern rebuke, "Boston, you seem to be more interested in watching people than building roads." I apologized profusely, but I have often wondered if that was God's way of calling me to go into the ministry.

I had been in a church and Sunday School since I joined the Baptist church. Since I had been in college, I was active in the Baptist Student Union on campus, which gave me some background in church life. It was on a Saturday night that I made my decision. My first question was, who could I tell who would understand? Mom and Dad had become inactive in their church. Mom now attended a small Christian Science church, which she had attended when she was growing up in Kansas City. I thought they might be more confused or amused rather than congratulatory. My roommate was at home for the weekend. He would be startled, but appreciative. Most of my fraternity brothers would have laughed out loud or maybe they would have hidden their snickering. I did not have a close girlfriend to tell. I thought of making an appointment with the chaplain of the university. I suspected that he would applaud my decision in an impersonal sort of way since he had not known me.

I knew I had to tell some human body. My relief and feelings of joy and enthusiasm were overflowing. I knew that such a decision needed to be shared. I could not wait much longer. I asked God who to tell. He didn't answer. I suppose He thought, That is something you need to figure out for yourself. I knew of one person who I thought would be glad to hear about my decision, and that was Jimmy Bailey, my best friend in high school and who himself already had decided to become a Methodist minister. Another person who would understand was Rev. Bill Jones.

The next morning, which was Sunday, I walked to the Sumter Highway, thumbed a ride to Sumter, and caught a Greyhound bus to Darlington. The bus station was one block from the church. The bus arrived at 10:55 a.m. At five after eleven I walked into the sanctuary and sat in the back pew. I had not slept the night before and was not dressed for church. In that day and time every woman, man, and child wore their Sunday best to church. I sang the hymns with gusto, but I did not hear a word of the sermon. When the last hymn was played and Reverend Jones walked down to the front pew to invite anyone who was being led to join the church, I walked briskly down the aisle to where he was standing. Before the music stopped, he whispered, "What are you doing here? You're supposed to be in school." I told him my reason for coming. He then told the congregation to sit down after the hymn. I still remember his very words: "Most of you know Bobby Boston. He has made the decision to go into the ministry." Suddenly there was a loud applause, and with tears in my eyes I felt like I had told the whole wide world. I remember I saw a tear on the side of Reverend Jones's eye, too.

The third life-changing event took place that summer in 1954 between my sophomore and junior year in college. I continued my summer job working with the tree company and was traveling throughout South Carolina and North Carolina during the week. One weekend while I was home, I heard some very sad news. My friend since the second grade, Rose Erwin, had broken up with Murray Yarborough, who she had been dating seriously since her senior year in high school. I could only imagine how devastating this could be for Rose. I called her up and invited her to go with me to hear an evangelist who was speaking at a church in Florence, South Carolina. The minister was Howard Bates, who we both had heard some five years earlier when we attended a church conference at Ridgecrest with the youth group. I sat with Rose in a large auditorium in Florence amidst hundreds of people, not hearing much of what was said. I pretended that I was listening, but actually my mind was on Rose. I was not thinking about what had happened between her and Murray but rather how comfortable I felt just being with her.

My first memory of Rose was when we both were in the second grade at St. John's Grammar School in Darlington. We were not in the same classroom but across the hall from each other. I remember thinking (as much as this eight-year-old could think), I bet that girl is really smart. She was always dressed a little neater than most of the other second-grade girls. She wore glasses and her long black hair was always neatly combed. I can recall seeing her from time to time as we grew up and thinking how good-looking she was, especially her legs.

While sitting there in that large auditorium I also remembered the night we were at a teenage party at Carolyn Stone's house playing Post Office. Rose picked me several times over the other boys, requesting a special-delivery stamp. From that day to this day, which spans more than sixty years, I have never forgotten the way she took off her glasses and looked up to me in the almost dark, opened her mouth, and taught me how to kiss. I also remember feeling kind of proud of myself that night.

Also, I felt some pride and the reality that here I was on the date with the girl who finished high school at the top of her class while I finished somewhere in the bottom half.

I cannot remember much of what happened after we left the evangelical service that evening in the summer of 1954, but I do recall that later that summer Rose went with me to enroll as a junior at Furman University as a ministerial student. Rose would be returning to Furman for her own junior year. We were back in school together, except the girls' campus was on one side of Greenville, and the boys' campus was on the other side.

I had wanted to stay at USC but my minister, Reverend Jones, and Rev. Harold Cole, who was the state youth director for the Southern Baptist Church, had strongly urged me to transfer to Furman in order to become acquainted with other ministerial students and the theology and traditions of the Southern Baptist Church. My undergraduate work at Furman will testify that this was one of the best decisions I would ever make. As a bonus, Rose would be there, too.

CHAPTER ELEVEN

MY FURMAN YEARS

Rose and I home from Furman, 1955

My transfer from USC to Furman was uneventful. I was glad to discover that all my grades from both Wofford and Carolina could be transferred. Because I had been in the School of Civil Engineering, I had more hours than I needed to be a junior. Another pleasant surprise: the tuition for Baptist ministerial students was half what other students had to pay.

Even though school expenses at Furman were less than at

Carolina, I still had to work to make ends meet. I found a part-time job at Liberty Insurance Company, working in the print shop, which was located about five blocks from the campus. I worked from 3 p.m. to 5 p.m., Monday through Friday, for 75 cents per hour. I decided to major in religion and psychology. I had the opportunity to transfer my membership in the SAE fraternity from USC to Furman, but I remembered what Reverend Jones had said about getting active in the Ministerial Association. Realizing I did not have time to be active in both, I chose the association, even though I personally preferred the other. Between classes, work, and special events at school, there was little time left for more pleasurable activities.

I saw Rose on the weekends, usually to go to a movie on Saturday night and church on Sunday morning. As the year progressed, I found myself wanting to be with her more often, which required a lot of walking since the main campus was about two miles from the women's campus. It seems in retrospect that my classes at Furman were more interesting and enjoyable than at Wofford or Carolina. I suppose that at Wofford my first interest was getting through class in order to practice football and at Carolina I was unsure as to how I was going to use all the math that I was taking.

I now had a goal and a purpose, which was to get a degree and go on to seminary. At Furman, I especially enjoyed my history

My father and I

classes with Dr. Winston Babb and religion classes with Dr. Henry Flanders and Dr. John Barry. I had only one class with Rose, as she majored in sociology. My junior year at Furman went by rather uneventfully. Neither Rose or I were interested in participating in the social life at Furman, mainly because on my part there was little time left over between work, classes, and study. We walked around downtown Greenville a lot and through the parks. Our relationship seemed to grow stronger week by week and I began to realize that Rose had the background and temperament to be a good minister's wife—that is, a good wife for a minister. It would take a while to find out if I was a good minister. She had always been active in her church and was an excellent pianist. I don't remember talking much about our relationship. It just seems to have grown naturally. We both were kind of shy.

There was one big disappointment in my junior year. That was my experience in the Ministerial Association, which Reverend Jones had strongly encouraged me to attend. We met for two hours every Wednesday night, which I thought was too long for the agenda. There was some social time in the beginning of the meeting and then the students had a prayer service focusing on those who were deemed sinners because they had a worldly life, such as drinking alcohol, smoking, and presenting liberal beliefs. I was guilty on most all these accounts. I was especially troubled when some of the names mentioned were faculty members, some of whom I had come to appreciate, and students who I had come to like. I began thinking, If this is what most Baptists believe, then I'm out of place. I began finding excuses to miss some of the meetings and eventually dropped out. I found out later that I was put on the prayer list.

As the summer between my junior and senior years approached, I had to decide what kind of work I could do for the summer. I could find a part-time job in Darlington, or continue my old summer job with the tree company. Before I could decide I got a call from Rev. Theron Anderson, the pastor of the First Baptist Church in Latta, South Carolina. He asked if I would be willing to serve as an intern for three months while he and his wife took a sabbatical to go to Europe to study and travel. It did not take long for me to say yes. I envisioned an opportunity to experience what it would be like to be a Baptist minister.

Latta is only forty miles from Darlington, about an hour drive through the country. Arrangements were made for me to stay in a local boarding house, which provided a room on the third floor and included a country-style breakfast and supper. Sandwiches for lunch were offered but were unnecessary because some member of the church always invited me to lunch, which was usually a five-course meal with an abundance of vegetables, as most residents of Lotta had vegetable gardens.

Latta is a relatively small town with a population of about four thousand, equally divided between "coloreds" and "whites." The coloreds lived on one side of town in unpainted houses with dirt lawns while most white folks lived in freshly painted homes with green-grass lawns and some kind of garden. Segregation was strongly enforced, which at the time was not an issue for me since I had grown up in Darlington where segregation was the accepted way of living by both races. There were colored restaurants and restaurants for the white folks. Filling stations had three restrooms on the side. One for men, one for women, and one for colored folks. White folks who could afford a maid always had an extra toilet located on the back porch. This was the summer of 1954.

I was excited! Not yet twenty-one, I was considered by the local clergy as a student minister, not yet licensed or ordained. Many of the townfolks and the members of the Latta Baptist Church called me "Preacher" and to remove any doubts about my new status in life, there it was in the Sunday bulletin, right next to "Sermon" and written for all to see: Rev. Robert W. Boston. I dressed for the part, wearing dark pants, white shirt, and tie. Since it was summer I saved my suit coat for Sunday.

My assigned duties during the week were to visit those who were shut in and unable to attend church on Sunday, those who had been reported as sick, or had been admitted to the hospital, which was located in the town of Dillon, about eight miles from Latta. I used Mom and Dad's old 1946 gray Plymouth to carry out my weekly pastoral duties. The hard and scary part of the summer assignment was to prepare three sermons, one for Sunday morning, another for Sunday evening, and still another for the Wednesday night prayer service. The frightening part about these assignments was that I had never preached a sermon, except for the one I had given for Youth Sunday at my church in Darlington. Nonetheless, I gained a lot of experience that would help me later.

As I began my senior year at Furman I was faced with three major tasks. One was to find a job where I could make enough to pay tuition, room, and board. The second was to decide what courses I needed to take to graduate, and the third was to decide how to handle my Baptist affiliation, since I continued to feel out of place. I had already applied to Southeastern Baptist Seminary in Winston-Salem, North Carolina, and had been accepted.

The first task was resolved when my hometown friend Jimmy Bailey, who was also working his way through Wofford college, told me about his job selling Electrolux vacuum cleaners. I visited the sales office in Greenville and was warmly accepted. I discovered that if I sold two vacuums a week I would make enough to pay for school and have enough extra to buy a used car, which was necessary to sell the vacuums. I was confident I could do that.

The second task was decided for me by administrative and faculty advisers.

The third task was not so easy and would take a few months to work out. It required a lot of mental and emotional toil, as well as soul searching. My three-month internship as a Baptist pastor in Latta was very positive and rewarding. I have learned since that the Latta Baptist Church, like the First Baptist Church in Darlington, was different from the majority of Southern Baptist churches. Both seemed open and affirming of different beliefs and lifestyles.

Rose joined me in visiting several Presbyterian churches in the Greenville area on Sundays. I had chosen to consider the Presbyterians because my father and mother had been members of the Presbyterian church in Darlington. The experience was most positive and encouraged me to continuing my efforts to become a minister.

During our Christmas break, I visited with Dr. Lilly, the minister at the First Presbyterian Church in Hartsville, South Carolina, and shared with him my dilemma. In his kind and gentle manner, he shared his personal experience in the church. He also loaned me several reading materials on the history and the beliefs of the Presbyterian Church. He suggested that I continue to visit other Presbyterian churches and have conferences with other ministers when there was an opportunity. He invited me to come back and bring Rose whenever we were home on the weekend. After several visits with Dr. Lilly, I felt ready to join the Presbyterian church.

But as I decided on this path I was confronted with another looming dilemma. How was I going to tell Reverend Jones, who had been my pastor, guide, mentor, and father figure since I was twelve years old? The thought of changing denominations seemed like I was disowning my own family. Yet, my resolve was firm. The difficulty was deciding when and how I was going to tell him. I knew it had to be soon because I was on the Ministerial Association's prayer list and I wanted to tell him in person.

I vividly remember the occasion even though it was more than sixty years ago. I had called him from school and told him that I had something important to tell him. He told me to come by his office at the church on Saturday morning. Saturday came too soon. I had figured out just how I was going to tell him, but when I was there I felt lost for words. He gave me a hug and sat down beside his desk. I sat in a chair facing him. I felt like the prodigal son who was about to tell his dad that he was leaving home forever and could he have his inheritance. I remember a lump in my throat and a flutter in my stomach as I talked about all the current activities at Furman until he interrupted me and said, "Bobby, you told me on the phone from school that you had something to tell me that was very important and what you have been telling me doesn't seem all that important."

What I said next seems blurry, except for the tears that began to flow. I think it was short and went something like this: "After spending a year at Furman, I have decided to join the Presbyterian Church. Instead of going to Southeastern Baptist Seminary, I'm going to attend Columbia Theological Seminary in Atlanta." Then there was a brief moment of silence, which felt like an hour or more. I wondered in the silence, Will he try to talk me out of my decision?

In the next moment he stood up, walked over, and stood beside my chair, with his aged, wrinkled hand on my shoulder. I think I saw wet in his eyes again, but then it may have been looking through the tears in my own. In his slow Virginian accent I remember him saying, "Bobby, I want to share something personal with you and I would like you to keep it to yourself. I am going to retire in just a few years and most people in these parts would not understand, but I believe you will. If I were going into the ministry in this day and time, I would become a Presbyterian, too." New tears within me began to flow but they were tears of a different flavor. Reverend Jones's secret remained joyfully in my heart until long after he died. Many years later I told this story to his son, an elementary-school principal in Anderson, South Carolina, and my doubles tennis partner in high school, only to find out that he too had been a Presbyterian for many years, served as an elder, and was instrumental in organizing a new Presbyterian church.

Now I was ready for another life-changing decision. Rose and I had been going together steadily for over a year and a half. It seemed that everything we did outside of our classes we did together. During the past year we had lived together almost like a married couple except we slept in separate beds, she on one side of Greenville and me on the other side. It was time to celebrate and make our relationship official with family and friends. I think it was during the Christmas holidays that I went to Wells Jewelers in Darlington and bought an engagement ring for $10.00 down and $10.00 a month for twelve months. I picked one of our evenings out, and at a given moment I took the ring out of the box and put it on her finger without saying a word. She seemed delighted but not surprised.

The next phase was to ask her mother's permission, or, as I like to think about it, her "blessings." Traditionally, that would have been the father's responsibility, but Rose's father had died when she was just a baby. This test seemed

My mother and I at my graduation from Furman, 1956

66

much more dif-
ficult than ask-
ing Rose if she
would marry
me. My uneasi-
ness resulted
from the aware-
ness that I was
not nearly as
stable as Mrs.
Zubie Erwin's
other son-in-
law, Carl, or her
own son, Pat.
I had gone to
three different
colleges, trying
to decide what I

Rose's mother Zubie, Rose, my father Elmo, my mother Peggy, and me, Furman graduation, 1956

wanted to do for the rest of my life. At the end of every
month I didn't have a penny to my name and it would be
three years before I would have a steady job. There was
the possibility I would be taking her youngest daughter
to some faraway place. And perhaps worst of all, I had
decided to leave the Baptist church and become a Presbyterian. I was not sure myself that I would want a daughter
of mine to marry someone whose future was so uncertain.

To my pleasant surprise her only response was, "I am
pleased. Do you have a date in mind?" I thought for sure
she would suggest we wait four or five years to set a time.
Rose and I had talked about June 22. That would be three
weeks after our graduation from Furman and three weeks
before classes were to begin at Columbia Seminary. We
returned to school for our final semester. I was excited! I
wanted to tell the whole world that I was getting married
on June 22. I thought to myself, "Now I have some stabil-
ity in my life." The stable part, of course, was Rose.

CHAPTER TWELVE

OUR WEDDING AND HONEYMOON

Cutting

Our wedding, 1956

The semester seemed to go quickly. I had only a few
courses to take. I was keeping pace selling two vacuum cleaners a week and some weeks three. My tuition was
waivered because the dean had asked if I would live in and
be a counselor in the new dormitory that had been built on
the new campus. Freshmen would live in the dorm and
be bused to the old campus for classes. I was driving my

old Plymouth, which was filled with vacuum cleaners. I felt rich and secure, probably for the first time since I had lived in a cradle and in my mother's arms.

Graduation could not come soon enough. My only disappointment was that since I did not have to pay for tuition, I thought I would have some money saved for a honey-

Wedded bliss

moon when graduation was over; actually, I was dead broke. But I had a plan. I figured what our wedding and honeymoon would cost, which included the tuxedo rental, the ring, and three nights in a hotel in Myrtle Beach, plus food and gas for the car. That meant I would need to sell six vacuums before June 22. So our plan was that I would stay in Greenville to sell the vacuums while Rose went home and planned the wedding. I assumed it would take most of the three weeks to sell six vacuum cleaners. In all the excitement, I sold six in the first week and a half. I could not wait to get home. A wiser person probably would have stayed the extra week, sold more, and had some money left over. But I had grown up with the reality that you were supposed to live paycheck to paycheck, with no money left over at the end of the month.

The wedding and reception were beautiful and went on without a hitch. Both sides of the family were there and it seemed like all of Darlington came out to celebrate with us. My dad stood by me as the best man, sober as a judge. Reverend Jones performed the ceremony.

Celebrating our 50th Wedding Anniversary, 2006

We had made reservations at the Latta Motel, which I had heard had a honeymoon suite. We finally arrived there a little before midnight. The room was decorated in all-white with a bouquet of red roses on the bedside table. We both were totally exhausted after the 8 o'clock wedding thirty miles away, but we woke up perky the next morning. The first thing I did on the first day of our marriage: I went out and tried to wipe off the white shoe polish that Billy Jones, the preacher's son, and some friends had painted on the old Plymouth. I really wanted to go on our honeymoon looking like an old married couple. When I went back to get Rose to go to breakfast, I was astonished to see that she had straightened the room, hung up the towels, made up the bed, and left it looking just like it was when we arrived. When I told her she didn't need to do that at a motel, she reminded me, "When you stay at someone's house you always leave it cleaner than you found it."

We went for breakfast at a small diner just across the street from the motel. When I started to pay the cashier she told me that our breakfast had been paid. When I looked around to see who might have done it, I saw a couple of old men sitting in a booth grinning. I asked her, "How did they know?" She said, "They saw you trying to wash the shoe polish off your car."

Myrtle Beach was about sixty miles from Latta. We thought we would get there in time to walk and sit on the beach before lunch, but about twenty miles out of Latta the engine on the old Plymouth began to smoke. I stopped beside the road, raised the hood and heard a hissing sound. Being an athlete and a pre-ministerial student, I didn't know what I was looking at or hearing. I got back in the car and slowly continued down the highway. As luck would have it, before long we ran up on a mechanic's shop just a few miles outside of the little town of Dillon. The gentleman who greeted us told us, without even looking under the hood, that we either had a busted hose or a bad water pump. When he did look, he informed us that it was both, and that he could replace them for about $25.00. That was what we had saved for two nights in a motel! Since we didn't have a choice, I told him to go ahead and fix the car, with the thought that we might have to go back to Darlington and spend the rest of our honeymoon with Rose's mother. Back in those days there were no credit cards or checks. It was cash or no go. Mournfully, I pulled the money out of my pocket when he had finished. Then the old mechanic looked at both Rose and me and said, "I see you've just got married, so the bill is on me." I took a deep breath, thanked him, and asked him, "How did you know?" His answer: "That was easy, there was white shoe polish that had dripped down the inside of the motor." I had received my first lesson on marriage. When you get married, let everybody you meet know about it. I felt rich again.

It was off again to the beach. At least we would have part of the afternoon to enjoy jumping in the waves and sunning on the sand. Back in the 1950s you didn't make hotel or motel reservations, you just drove until you saw a pleasant-looking place with a vacancy sign on the window or the marquee. We found one we liked just two blocks from the beach. I think it was called the Dogwood or something like that. We didn't even consider a beachfront accommodation because it would have cost twice as much. We had two beautiful days staying in a luxury motel, swimming, and walking on the beach, and making love in the nighttime. There was only one kink. On the second night, we had decided to go to a fancy restaurant for a seafood dinner, since it looked like our money was holding out. When the crab that Rose ordered was served it was obviously blackened and burnt. I told her we needed to send it back. She insisted that she was going to eat it. I learned another Erwin family rule: "If someone puts food on your plate, you eat all of it whether you like it or not."

Our honeymoon was about to end. We decided to stay on the beach our last day, as long as there was daylight, and then drive home at night. The car was packed and we sat on our blanket at the beach, wishing we could scrape enough out of our budget to stay another night. But it just was not possible. What little we had was to be used for our trip to Atlanta and the first month's rent on our one-room efficiency apartment.

While we were enjoying our last moments at the beach, a saggy-looking, unshaved old man with a walking stick came by. He remarked, "You young folks seem to be enjoying yourselves. Where are you from?" I was a little suspicious of him, but he seemed harmless. He probably just wanted to have a closer look at Rose's legs, which were well tanned after two days at the beach. He kept asking questions and we kept answering them, I suppose because we were kind of proud of what we had accomplished together and what we were about to accomplish. After about twenty minutes he knew everything about us and we knew nothing about him and were not particularly interested in him. Before he left, he made us a somewhat unbelievable offer.

He said that his house was only three blocks from the beach, and it was well furnished and even had some food in the refrigerator. He then invited Rose and me to stay in his house for a week since he was going to be away for a week or so beginning that night. I was now getting more suspicious and Rose even more than I. We told him, "Thanks, but no thanks, we need to get home." He then took out a piece of paper with his name, address, and phone number, and gave it to us. He said, "If you change your mind, give me a call." Rose and I couldn't help thinking about how nice it would be to spend a few more days here at the beach. Out of curiosity we drove by the address that he had been given to us and it was an attractive home.

The old fellow had mentioned that he was a member of the First Presbyterian Church, after I told him I was going to a Presbyterian seminary. Out of more curiosity I decided to call the church and ask the minister if he knew the man. Fortunately, the minister was there, and his immediate response was, "Why, that's old Charlie, one of the finest gentlemen you'll ever meet. He's been a member of this church for years and was elected elder for several terms." When I told him about his offer to stay in his house, he told me that was one of Charlie's good deeds. Being a widower in his eighties he owned several homes and enjoyed inviting people to use them.

The next phone call was to our previously unknown stranger. I told him we would like to take him up on his offer. He responded, "You have the address, enjoy yourself, and call me if you need anything." When we went inside his house everything was just as he said, well furnished, three bedrooms, two baths, a refrigerator and pantry full of food. We danced with joy.

I then had another idea. My grandmother, who we all called Gonga, had come all the way from Kansas City to be at our wedding. Except for pictures she had never seen the

Atlantic Ocean. We both agreed how good it would be to invite her to join us for our last few days. We had the room and plenty of food. I called her. The next morning, she got on a Greyhound bus and was there for lunch. That is the long story of how we happened to take our grandmother on our honeymoon.

Honeymoon with my grandmother Neil Tabler

CHAPTER THIRTEEN

Seminary Days

When Rose and I got back to Darlington, we had just a few days to pack up our stuff and head for Decatur, Georgia, our first home away from home. Rose had already found a job as a secretary at the Trust Company of Georgia, one of the largest banks in Atlanta. We had enough money saved to pay our first month's rent, and by the end of the first month Rose would have received her first paycheck and that would pay for the next month's rent, food, and gas. Though I wasn't making any money, I was feeling rich again.

We left Darlington to find our new home around the first of July, pulling a U-Haul trailer with all of our life's possessions, most of which were wedding gifts. I had bought a used 1952 Chevrolet from my dad because I did not believe the old Plymouth would make it to Atlanta and back. He signed a loan for us at the South Carolina National Bank in Darlington.

There was no one to welcome us to our first home. The apartment was small but quite adequate—one room with a double bed in a corner, the kitchen sink, an ice box in another corner, and a small living space in another corner. The bathroom and closet were off to the side in another small room. We were excited, and celebrated with each other.

It did not take us long to settle in. Rose had to go to work the next day and I had to enroll in an accelerated course in Greek and Hebrew at the seminary. Rose had discovered that she could catch the city bus right in front of our apartment that would take her directly to the Trust Company's front door. Columbia Seminary was only about four blocks from the apartment and I could drive there in minutes. Since we had not met any friends, we felt as if we were living in a world of our own. Every evening I met Rose's bus; we had supper on our little enamel table that Rose had brought from home; and we listened to the radio, especially *Amos 'n' Andy*. Then Rose went to bed early and I studied Greek and Hebrew. Our night out—or "date night," as we had come to call it—was to go to the local drive-in movie, where we ate hot dogs and French fries, drank Coca-Cola, and had a candy bar or Moon Pie for dessert. On weekends, we toured the sights of Atlanta, especially the big homes, and went to different churches on Sunday. We knew the routine would soon change, but for the present we enjoyed our new way of living.

Seminary living was good, though it included a lot of long hours, working and studying. There was very little social life since the students usually spent fifteen to eighteen hours six days a week studying and meeting the requirements of Greek, Hebrew, studies in the Old and New Testament, and church history.

In contrast, Rose, along with most seminary wives, worked in the real world, eight hours a day, or ten hours including the bus time. There was no school on Monday, giving students who served churches time to get back to school. Since Rose was working, I used my day off to play golf. A group of students and professors teamed up and played most Mondays. Rose sometimes complained that I had a day off and she didn't. She worked on Saturday, cleaning our one room, and if you think it should not take a whole day to clean one room, you don't know Rose.

There was no school in the summers, but for most students that was the time to find a real job that would pay enough to cover the tuition due in September. The first summer I tried selling cookware door to door, as I had with vacuum cleaners in college. After two weeks, I had not made enough to pay for my gas, so I quit and applied for a job as a lifeguard at a local swimming pool. I was hired and kept that job for two summers.

Life at the seminary did not change much over my three years except I did feel smarter and wiser from year to year. Like today, the faculty and students were divided between conservative and liberal views or somewhere in between. There was not a lot of discussion in the classes as to who was on which side. Those discussions took place in the halls, dormitories, and the dining room. Everybody seemed to know where everybody else stood on various issues facing the church. Looking back, I think most students came to seminary basically set with their views, based on their family backgrounds and the churches where they were raised. I think in many ways the seminary helped us polish what we thought.

I was on the liberal side, or what I would like to call the progressive side, and I could trace my position to Mother and Dad. They both were open and fair-minded when it came to world and community issues. My dad had an old saying that he repeated often, "There is enough good in the best of us and enough bad in the worst of us, it behooves any of us not to criticize another." I never heard either of them say anything derogatory about another person. Mother's advice about other folks was, "If you can't find something good to say about someone, don't talk about them."

My views on race relations developed early in my life. I remember a time when Dad managed a Shell gas station. Traditionally, most filling stations had three restrooms on the side, clearly marked MEN, WOMEN, and COLORED. Dad removed the COLORED sign and used the room to store old tires. When a colored person asked him where the colored restroom was, he told him, "You're a man, aren't you?" and pointed him to the side of the building. When the Darlington town council was made aware of Dad's restroom policy, several members (all white men) visited the station and told him, "Elmo, we just don't do things like that in this town." I never heard anything about the final outcome, but Dad never took out the tires nor did he turn away any colored person.

Seminary life was good and rich in spiritual growth and self-understanding, but the best part of these first three years of marriage was the other life we lived. We had been invited to conduct services at a small Presbyterian church in Wayside, Georgia, which was about an hour-and-a-half drive from Decatur. We were excited, but also quite nervous, having been told that if they liked us they might invite me to be their minister while we were still at the seminary.

Community Presbyterian Church had only thirty members, which was too small to call a full-time minister, so for years they had relied on student ministers who would come until he graduated. I spent several days and many hours preparing my trial sermon. I remember Rose's encouragement, "Just be yourself." Fortunately, we were invited to come back. The remuneration was $35.00 a Sunday, plus a good country meal. My job description was to lead the worship service and, in the afternoon, visit those who were sick, shut in, or in the hospital. I wrote my sermon on Saturday night, and was sometimes up until two or three in the morning. We then left Decatur at 8 o'clock and arrived in time for Sunday School at 9:30.

It was the beginning of three years of weekends, learning, loving, and laughter. Since we were younger than most of the adults, we felt as if we were being adopted by grandmothers and grandfathers, aunts and uncles, something we did not have growing up in Darlington. We were taught about cows, goats, horses, freezing on a deer stand (not to shoot but to see), frog gigging, and rowing a boat fast enough to outrun a copperhead.

An unfortunate incident took place several months after I began my ministry in Wayside. It was on a Sunday following the worship service and Sunday dinner. I had been informed that our Sunday School superintendent was ill, which explained why he was not in church, so I decided to visit him at home. He lived down a dirt road about two miles from the main highway on a small farm.

When I went to his house, I was met by his young daughter, who told me that her mother and dad were out in the barn and were expecting me. I noticed that there were several cars parked behind the barn. When I tried to open the barn door, I found that it was locked. I knocked and the superintendent, I will call him Jim, opened the door. As he did, I heard a lot of clatter behind him, like metal hitting metal. Jim was wearing overalls and announced rather loudly, "The preacher is here." Then he hesitantly said, "Come on in." I knew several of the men and women who were there and I immediately smelled a strong odor of alcohol. I realized I had walked into a liquor still.

Struggling to find the right words to introduce myself without sounding judgmental, I responded, "I have never seen a whiskey still. Could you show me how it works?" Jim mumbled a few remarks that I don't remember and then asked, "Would you like to go over to the house?" Feeling relieved, we went to the house. After a few moments of casual conversation about the church and Jim's recovery from illness, I decided it was time to leave. As I left, Jim said, "I will see you in church next Sunday." I told Rose on our way back to Atlanta, "I have never been so embarrassed both for myself and my Sunday School superintendent." Unfortunately, that was not the end of the story.

The next Sunday, elder Mac Davis said that he wanted to speak to me after worship service. When I met with him he told me with a grin that everyone in Wayside was talking about "the preacher who walked in on the liquor still." He also remarked, "You may have a decision to make." He further informed me that a federal law had recently been passed that stated that anyone who knows the location of a still and does not report it to the Bureau of Alcohol, Tobacco, and Firearms could be arrested as an accomplice, and that if I reported the site of the still I would receive a sizable reward.

He also told me that if I felt a need to report it, I would probably need to resign as minister of the church because of the number of members of the church who used that still. I had not been taught in seminary how to deal with such a problem.

Bob and his 1ˢᵗ Church

On Monday morning, I reported the incident to the president of the seminary. After laughing, he said that we needed to discuss the matter with the school's lawyer. In a phone call with the attorney, he too laughed and asked me a number of questions, specifically whether Jim had asked me to talk to him about the still. When I told him no, he said I would have to make the decision.

Rose and I pondered and prayed over this dilemma for

several days. On one hand, known crimes needed to be reported; and the reward for reporting the liquor still would be sufficient to pay our school tuition for the three years with a good amount left over for other needs. On the other side, we had bonded with the congregation. We loved the people and had enjoyed having dinner in almost every member's home. We were learning and enjoying country living. The people seemed to like us. We returned to Wayside the next Sunday and continued our ministry for the next three years as if nothing had happened. No federal agent ever came calling. I guess that means I have been a federal fugitive for the last half century.

It was hard to leave Wayside after three years. Even though we lived there only one day a week, we felt a part of the community and the lives of those who lived there. Rose summed up our experience when she suggested, "Why don't you get a part-time job and continue to be the minister of the Community Presbyterian Church in Wayside?"

1957, Wayside Church

CHAPTER FOURTEEN

ORDINATION AND MY FIRST FULL-TIME JOB

1959, Rose (pregnant with Robin) and I at my graduation
from Seminary

As the last quarter of my senior year approached, I knew it was decision time as to where we were going from there. Having spent a semester during my senior year as an intern chaplain at Georgia Baptist Hospital in Atlanta I had made the decision to go into hospital chaplaincy. Providing pastoral care seemed more appealing to me than having to write a sermon every Sunday.

I made an application to Grady Memorial Hospital in Atlanta to become a fellow in their three-year residential program to become a hospital chaplain. This sounded like an ideal situation for Rose and me. I would have a small salary and be able to continue our ministry at the Wayside Church. Rose would be able to keep her job at the Trust Company of Georgia. Best of all, we could stay in our apartment in Decatur and continue our association with Columbia Seminary. Three weeks later we received a letter from Chaplain Charles Gerkin, the chief chaplain, that we had been accepted into the residential program. Our only reservation was that we would have to wait three years to start a family, which we already had been discussing. We were excited and began sharing the news with our family and friends.

Several weeks later I experienced my first major disappointment in life. Chaplain Gerkin called me into his office and told me he had chosen another minister to replace me to balance the residential program on a cultural and ethnic basis. Instead, he had arranged a position for me in a residential program at Elgin State Hospital in Elgin, Illinois, which was at that time one of the highest recognized mental institutions in the nation, second only to the Memminger Clinic in Kansas. This was simultaneously a rejection and an honor.

It was decision time again. This would mean another temporary move. Rose would have to find another job. We would have to leave our church in Wayside and move farther away from our family and friends into an unknown world. We pondered, prayed, and cried. We were at one of our first critical crossroads in life. But now there was no minister, parent, or faculty advisor to advise us. Only God would know what would be best for us, but He was not talking. We were on our own. Lost but not alone.

It was the end of February. Graduation was only three months away. Students were discussing the churches they had been called to serve. I still had not made a commitment to go to Elgin State Hospital. What I didn't know was that there would be other choices to consider.

Late one evening I was walking down the main hall of the Columbia Seminary after I had been in the library looking for a sermon idea for Sunday. I stopped at the bulletin board, which usually had notices for job opportunities. I was struck by one in particular. It was a handwritten note by Rev. Joe Ledford from the Southminster Presbyterian Church in Kansas City, Missouri, stating that he would be at the seminary on a day in early March and would like to interview any student who would be interested in an assistant position. Please call this number. I took the note home to Rose. I felt a spark of interest. Kansas City was the place where I was born and where my extended family still lived—grandparents, aunts, uncles, and cousins, who I barely knew. I was seven years old when we moved to Darlington, to return to Kansas City for only two brief visits.

Rose gave me that "You can't be serious" look but I couldn't help being a little excited. Being an assistant in a large congregation had been my second choice to a chaplaincy position. I told Rose that it might be fun just to meet someone from Kansas City, so I called Reverend Ledford. He gave me a date as to when he would be at the seminary and offered to take Rose and me to dinner. We had a delightful steak dinner in one of Atlanta's finest restaurants, a treat Rose and I had never before experienced. He told us all about the church and some of the changes that had happened in the city since our family had moved away in 1939. As the evening ended, he extended an invitation for us to visit the church and the city with all expenses paid and no obligation. Rose could not go because of her work at the bank, so I went alone.

One day in early March 1959 I boarded a TWA flight to Kansas City. It was my first air flight. I was met at the airport by my grandparents, aunts, uncles, and cousins. It was an exciting week, a chance to see how a big church operated, and a delightful family reunion. Best of all, I was offered my first full-time job.

On my return, Rose met me at the airport, still with that look. I was experiencing a flood of emotions, thoughts, and possibilities. Reverend Ledford, Joe, had asked if I would call him soon, as he had some other prospects. In the next several days we talked a lot about our future, along with the pros and cons about where we would go from there. We had already had our plans settled for the next three years, but now they were all up in the air again. I had the thought that if we accepted the position in Kansas City, we could pay our education loans and be out of debt, have another church experience, and seek a chaplaincy residential program at a later date. A bonus was that we could start our own family sooner than we had planned. Rose shared the thought, "That all this sounds good, but I don't want to go any farther from Darlington than we are now."

What to do?

On June 5, 1959, with our 1957 Chevrolet filled with all our worldly possessions and Rose four months pregnant, we headed out west with that old song playing in my heart, "Kansas City, here I come, right back where I started from." You can imagine all of the emotions and thoughts that swirled in our minds and hearts as we traveled across the country to a new home, far from our old home. Our first stop was Paducah, Kentucky, where we spent the night at the Holiday Inn and first discovered "Western time," which was two hours earlier that Eastern time. I changed my watch, but Rose said that she was never going to change hers from Darlington time. Neither of us slept that night, wondering what the next day would be like.

As we drove into Kansas City, our first experience was of

intense heat, especially since our car didn't have an air conditioner. We stopped at a restaurant to eat and get cool. We had made arrangements to spend the first few nights at my Aunt Doris and Uncle Ed's home in Kansas City, Kansas, about twenty-five minutes from the Southminster Presbyterian Church. My aunt and uncle said we could stay with them until we found a place of our own. Our first night in Kansas City we had an exciting and enjoyable supper with my family. The plan was to meet Joe Ledford at the church on Monday morning.

Southminster was the second-largest Presbyterian church in Kansas City, with approximately fifteen hundred members. I would be the first assistant minister in the church's history. My job description was to work with the youth program, to assist the senior minister in visitations, and take part in the Sunday morning worship service. Since I was to meet Joe on Monday morning to begin my orientation and first day on the payroll, I decided to add a little mystery before beginning work. We went to worship services at Southminster on Sunday and sat in the back of the sanctuary incognito. At the end of the service we were greeted warmly as visitors and prospective members. I remember thinking that I was going to enjoy this congregation.

My first week was orientation in the history of the church and the plans for the future, youth programs, scheduled meetings, and, surprisingly, certain rules I was expected to follow in visiting church members. Joe, as I soon learned, was highly organized, methodical, and controlling, much like a CEO in a large company or a commanding officer of an army battalion. One of the rules for me, which I did not always follow, was that I should talk to him before visiting the homes of any parishioners. We had a staff meeting scheduled every morning to cover what Joe expected me to do. The staff consisted of Joe, the secretary, a custodian, and me. I began to realize that Joe's demeanor, as I experienced it in my initial interview and visit in his home, was strikingly different from our working relationship. But offsetting my discomfort in our initial working relationship, there were many positives.

I wanted to learn the ins and outs of church administration and Joe was one of the best. I liked the way he conducted the Sunday worship service and I enjoyed his sermons, which were theologically sound and spiced with humor, a side of him I did not see outside of the worship hour. I soon found myself immersed in the youth program, a part of the church life that I had never experienced as an adult. From the toddlers in the nursery to the seniors in high school, I became thoroughly engulfed. Joe seemed pleased and admitted that he was not very comfortable with young people. I had noticed he was a strict disciplinarian with his own two children. I enjoyed the summer youth camps and teaching a Sunday School class for seventh and eighth graders.

We had found a house to rent about a mile from the church. It was a two-story home that was owned by an elderly widow named Mary Jane Lampking. She lived on one side and we lived on the other. We enjoyed buying furniture to set up a room for our baby, expected sometime in November. Also, there were the many activities that were being planned by our long-lost-and-found extended family. My dad's side of the family lived in Kansas City; Mother's side lived in Independence, Missouri, on the other side of the Missouri River. We enjoyed frequent cookouts and dinners on both sides. It did not take long to catch up on the last twenty years.

Almost every evening when there was not a church meeting, we visited one branch of our family or another. My maternal grandfather, Silas Austin, who I had always known as Bobo, taught Rose and me how to play bridge. He and his second wife, Erma, lived in Kansas City, not far

Me, my sister Joy, my father, and my brother Ronnie, 1958

from the church. Bobo was the one who sent me the $200 to pay my tuition at USC so I would not volunteer for the draft during the Korean War. Bobo was the wealthiest member of both the Austin and Boston families. He had been the owner of one of the largest printing companies in Kansas City. Rose and I enjoyed our monthly bridge games.

My maternal grandmother, who I called Gonga, lived with her daughter Jean in Independence. She was the one who bought and made my clothes before I was six years old and moved to South Carolina. I have always felt close to her, as she came to South Carolina at least once a year. She was the grandmother who went with Rose and me on our honeymoon.

Most of our family time was spent at Aunt Doris and Uncle Ed's. My paternal grandmother Bertha Boston, who I called Nana, and my cousin Donnie also lived there. We spent many evenings there playing cards, either Hearts or Spades, and talking about life in the 1930s, before I was seven years old. Rose seemed to fully enjoy her new extended family. Growing up in Darlington, neither Rose nor I had had an extended family to enjoy. There were moments when I felt a tinge of guilt, thinking, Did I accept the call

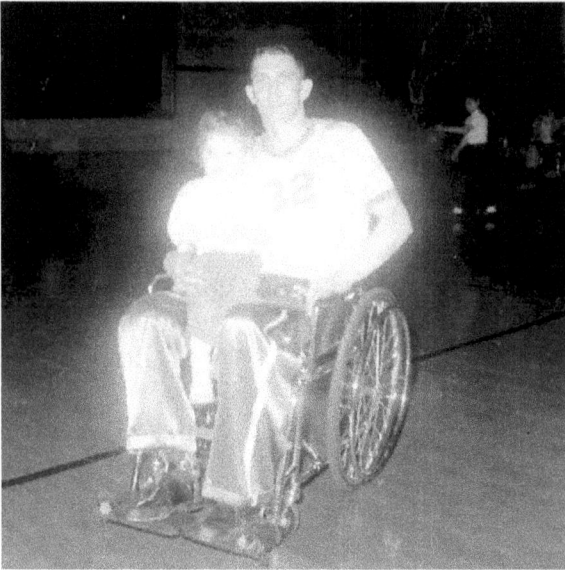

Donnie and Robin around 1960

to Southminster Presbyterian Church just to get to be with my own grandparents, aunts, uncles, and cousins?

The one member of the family with whom I developed the closest relationship was my cousin Donnie. He was living at home with his mother and dad (Aunt Doris and Uncle Ed) in a hospital bed. He was completely paralyzed from the waist down from a gunshot wound. Donnie had been an outstanding athlete. He lettered in three sports in high school, football, basketball, and track, and went to Concordia University in Nebraska on a basketball scholarship. During his sophomore year, Donnie, a monitor in his dormitory, had attempted to get a student to stop throwing beer cans down the hall. When Donnie turned around to go back to his room the student shot Donnie in the back, severing all the nerves leading to his legs. He had spent four months in intensive care in the Concordia Hospital, not expected to live and too vulnerable to transfer to a hospital near his home in Kansas City. When we arrived, he had been home for only a few weeks. His doctors reported that Donnie had made a miraculous recovery but because of the extent of his internal injuries, he probably would not live past the age of thirty-six. This for me was the beginning of a long and lifetime friendship.

With all of the church activities and family get-togethers, it seemed that my first year was passing fast. The biggest and most exciting event was the birth of our daughter Robin, who was born on November 24, 1959 at St. Luke's Hospital, only a few blocks from St. Mary's, where I was born. All went well except that because of Rose's long labor—twenty-four hours—I was so nervous I could not stay in the delivery room for long. Donnie came to the hospital in his wheelchair and alternated with me rubbing Rose's back.

I continued to enjoy my work at the church, but there were some tensions. Contrary to Joe's rule that I was to call him before I visited in the home of a parishioner, I was beginning to receive calls from church members to come to their home for a visit with the request that I not tell Joe. This became an opportunity to provide some pastoral counseling, which was my major in seminary, but I felt torn about whether to tell Joe. And I was disappointed that Joe never invited me to conduct Sunday services, even when he was away. He always called an elderly minister. I suspected

Donnie and I at a family reunion, 1995

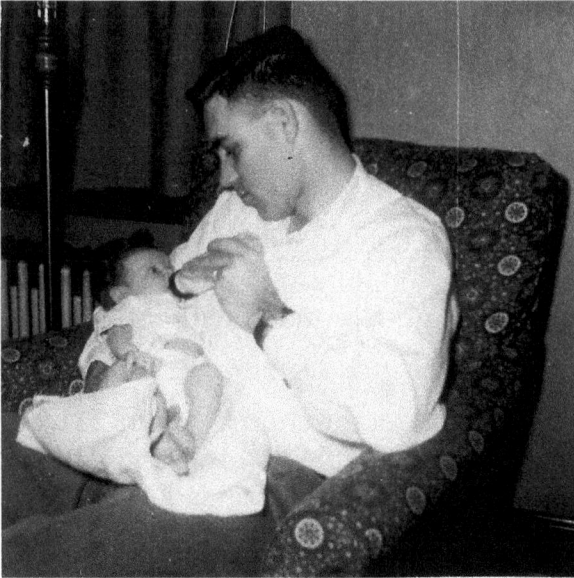

Me holding Robin, age two months, 1959

that this was because of his possessiveness of the church members. However, I really did not mind much because this left me free to enjoy the weekend with my own family.

During what was to be my first and only year at Southminster, I had a frightening experience. It happened the first week of February 1960. One of the disappointments for Rose and me was the lack of snow during the first two months of the winter. In discussing the pros and cons of moving to Kansas City, one of the pros was to experience snowfalls. We had been told that Kansas City had numerous snowstorms during the winter months. Normally, the first storm could be expected before Thanksgiving. We had prepared ourselves with boots, sleds, snow shovels, and hooded jackets to survive and enjoy the snow. Rose and I had experienced only a few snowfalls our entire lives, and those melted before we could play in them. So, by September we were ready for snow.

Thanksgiving came and no snow had fallen. Christmas and New Year's went by and still no snow. Weather forecasters were astounded. Weather records for the latest first snow of the year were broken. Everyone we knew was delighted, except for Rose and me. Then it happened. On

February 7, 1960, a massive snowstorm hit Kansas City and the neighboring communities. One to two feet of snow covered the city. The National Guard had to be activated. Schools, churches, and most offices were closed. Everyone was advised to stay in their homes until the cleaning crews could open the streets. Rose and I went out in the streets to play. The city was paralyzed. Rose and I remember looking out the window and thinking, "How beautiful."

One week later, as the city was in the process of recovering, another storm, just as devastating, arrived. By then, even Rose and I were getting tired of the snow. According to weather records, Kansas City had more snow the month of February 1960 than at any time in its history.

Then one Sunday morning following the last snowfall, Joe Ledford in jest said to the congregation, "Did you know that our assistant minister and his wife have been praying for snow all winter? I think it is time for them to stop, don't you?" Laughter followed. This would have been the end of it except for the fact that the services were broadcast throughout the city and surrounding communities. When Rose and I got home that afternoon our phone didn't stop ringing. There were calls filled with anger and threats. We considered changing our phone number. The following week I was getting a haircut in a local barbershop when a large barrow-chested man stood up and asked me if I was the assistant minister at Southminster who had been praying for this snow we had been having. I smiled and said, "That is the story being told." He then began to cuss and shake his fist at me. I feared for a moment that he was going to hit me! I think he might have if the barber had not stood between him and me. I cannot help feeling sad that many people believe that one man's prayers can change the weather. I thought later that the first time I had the opportunity to deliver a sermon I would name it, "Can Our Prayers Change the Weather?"

As the snow melted and spring began to arrive, our lives returned to normal, but I was about to make a change. At some time in the early spring I received a call from the chairman of the pulpit nominating committee of the Northminster Presbyterian Church in Kansas City, asking if I would consider meeting with the committee. I did and after several meetings I accepted a call to become minister of the church beginning the first of June.

I had enjoyed working with the youth and the members of Southminster, but my relationship with Joe continued to decline. I had learned a lot about church organization from him but became more and more uncomfortable with his form of leadership. The farewell reception was welcomed but sad. I would miss those I had come to know and love, especially the youth of the church.

CHAPTER FIFTEEN

NORTHMINSTER PRESBYTERIAN CHURCH

Robin, me, Rose, and my mother in Kansas City, 1962

The move from Southminster to Northminster went smoothly, with a borrowed trailer loaded with our new baby bed and high chair, along with the chair and mattress. Northminster was located about fifteen miles through the city and across the Missouri River in a recently developed suburb known as Kansas City North. The church was only two years old and had recently moved into the first phase of a building program for a fellowship hall, Sunday School rooms, a kitchen, and the minister's and secretary's offices. Rev. Gray Dashon, the organizing pastor, had retired. It was an ideal setting. The church also owned a manse located a block away. It did not take long with a substantially increased salary to buy all new furniture.

The congregation had 157 members, most around the age of Rose and me, with a good number of children and a few senior citizens. There were six ruling elders and eight deacons. I remember my first day at work, sitting in my new office chair feeling a sense of grandeur along with a heavy feeling of responsibility. It was left up to me to decide where to begin. My mission was to lead the congregation and its continued growth in development by visiting and getting to know personally the families in the church and prospective members in the community, along with serving as a member of the building committee of the church, which was already visualizing a new sanctuary. And along with these matters was writing a sermon for Sunday services.

I had learned a lot from Joe Ledford about church organization. I visualized being a teaching minister, not a preacher, and that I would guide the church officers and members to decide what they needed and where to go from there. I am a strong believer in what the apostle Peter said about "the priesthood of all believers," which suggests that all who follow the teachings of Jesus are ministers in their own way. My calendar filled quickly and stayed full. I most enjoyed receiving new members into the church, infant baptisms, conducting marriage ceremonies, and counseling couples who were planning their marriages. My least enjoyable experience was having to write a sermon every Sunday. I found the members of Northminster for the most part progressive and open to new ways of thinking, and exploring different ways to serve the community. They accepted people of different nationalities, race, religions, and lifestyles. Differences of thinking were dealt with openly and discussed freely. There were conservative members who blended well with the more progressive members. I was discovering that the midwestern Presbyterians were more progressive than southern Presbyterians.

During my first week at the church I made a visit that taught me a lesson that has lasted throughout my ministry. In my first meeting with the officers of the church I was asked to call on a woman named Ruth Adams, who was bedridden in her home with a diagnosis of a fourth-stage cancer with only a few months to live. I remember parking in front of her house and wondering what I could say to someone who knew that she was dying. I did not learn that in seminary or in my tenure as a chaplain at Georgia Baptist Hospital. I remember the relief I felt when I rang the doorbell, and no one came to the door.

Then two days later, when I returned, a nurse answered the door and led me into Ruth's room. After a few words of introduction, the nurse left the room. I sat down on the chair by her bed and after a few moments of silence I said, "Mrs. Adams, I don't know what to say." Then she in a quiet and strong voice said, "Dear, you don't have to worry about that, I will tell you what to say. First, call me Ruth, not Mrs. Adams, and then tell me about your family and how you happened to come to Northminster." That was the beginning of many meaningful and delightful visits. She taught me that when I visit someone, I don't have to worry about what to say. I can let them tell me by asking, "How can I be helpful?"

I remember only two incidents that caused any conflict in the church. Really, both seemed as if they would result in conflict, but didn't. One was when the session of the church agreed to have a pulpit and choir exchange with an African American church. This was in 1963, with segregation between the races practiced in all parts of the city. I enjoyed the experience and was told that some members who had opposed the exchange had attended anyway and enjoyed the experience. The black minister was Cecil Williams, one of the leaders of the civil rights movement, who participated in the 1965 Selma to Montgomery marches.

The second event was my own doing. I had been at the church for almost three years and was amazed at how many people attended church on Easter Sunday. Our average attendance was around two hundred, which was the capacity of the new fellowship hall, which had been turned into a sanctuary. On Easter Sunday the attendance was three times greater. We had arranged to have three services, at 8:30, 10, and 11:30 a.m. I started early in the week preparing my sermon and by 1 a.m. Sunday I felt I had prepared an exceptionally good Easter sermon. Then I had what I remember thinking was an inspiration, a divine inspiration. Rose called it "The devil talking." The sermon came last in the service, following the choir's anthem and before the last hymn. I had decided that instead of giving them my sermon on Easter morning I would reserve the sermon until the Sunday after Easter.

Here is how it happened. I remember the words to this day. I began my sermon, "I am glad you have joined us for our Easter celebration. I suspect some of you are hoping for a short sermon and I have one for you. I have written what I think is a good sermon, but I realize the most important part of Easter is the Sunday after, for this is the Sunday we begin to decide what Easter means in our daily living. So, I've decided to hold my sermon until next Sunday. Let us stand for our final hymn."

The choir members looked stunned. I did not look at the congregation. Following that hymn I walked to the back of the sanctuary, gave the benediction, walked out the back door, and went home to wait for the second service. Since there was only about a half hour between the services, no one knew about no sermon except the choir and they were sequestered in the choir room.

The following week was quiet. I planned to take a few days away following Easter. I did not know what to expect when I returned for the worship service the following Sunday. To my surprise, the sanctuary was filled to capacity and people were standing in the back and on the sides.

Following the service, several people expressed an interest in joining the church. The good news was that I was not asked to look for another church and some folks even told me that the sermon, last Sunday's Easter sermon, was one of the best they had ever heard. I felt redeemed. Rose still thought otherwise.

A worthwhile adventure while we were in Kansas City and one that would be life-changing was my standing in the National Guard. I had joined the National Guard when I was a junior in high school, along with several class-mates. My service in the Guard had been deferred while I was in college and seminary. In my third year at North-minster I received a letter from the U.S. government in-forming me that I needed to request a discharge or return to active duty. When I responded that I was a Presbyterian minister serving a church in Kansas City, the government replied that I would be eligible for an appointment to be a chaplain upon approval of the U.S. Presbyterian Church and a willingness to attend the U.S. Army Chaplains' School, located in New York City. After numerous letters and phone calls and discussions I accepted the appoint-ment. I went from being a buck private to a first lieuten-ant in the Missouri National Guard. My only requirement was to spend eight hours a month with a National Guard unit. The congregation seemed to be well pleased with my extra-curricular duties. My visits to Guard units were en-joyable, almost like being a member of a civic club and getting paid to attend.

The weekends (after church services) were usually spent visiting one of our extended families or trying to locate one of the dozen or so houses our family had lived in be-fore we moved to Darlington. My mother sent pictures of the houses/apartments. The reason for moving so many times, she explained, was due to our country's Depression. As our family expanded and our finances fell, we needed to find another place to live. Rose did not enjoy the house

Donnie and me in Kansas City

search. She liked to ride by the city's mansions.

Some of my most enjoyable times were with my cousin Donnie. When he became mobile, using his wheelchair, he could do whatever he wanted. Instead of going back to college he went to a stenography school and became a court reporter and worked for the state of Kansas judicial system for more than thirty-five years. He played wheelchair basketball and always drove a Cadillac convertible with hand controls. We enjoyed going to Kansas City Chiefs football games and Kansas City Royals baseball games. He had free admission and I got in free too if I pushed his wheelchair. I remember him saying, "I'll play crippled, you do the pushing." If they had only known that Don could get upstairs and downstairs as well as I could with two good legs.

One other exciting adventure with Donnie was seeing my first XXX movie. One of the theaters in Kansas City advertised a movie entitled *I Am Curious (Yellow)*. This caused an uproar among all the churches in both Kansas and Missouri. The Supreme Court of Kansas made arrangements to attend the movie on a designated morning to determine its appropriateness. Donnie was the appointed court reporter. Before they went to the show, Donnie suggested to the court that it would be good to have a minister join them for the showing and that he knew a minister who would be willing to attend. The judge sent me a formal invitation. I was excited to see something I had never seen before. [Bob's family remembers that he wouldn't let Rose view the film.]

Since Donnie and I both had a competitive streak from our athletic days we found many games to compete with each other. There was croquet, Jarts, pool, and sometimes just throwing cards into a hat. Donnie won most of them.

The most sterling event of our Northminster days was the birth of our son Russell Erwin Boston on February 20, 1962. For historic reference he was the first child born to a minister of the church. He was a celebrated baby as the congregation showered him with gifts, but his birth was notable for other reasons, too. On the night before he was born there was a snowstorm. We had already put chains on our tires in case Rose had to go to the hospital. But it was the next night at about 9 o'clock when her water broke, signaling that it was time to go. My mother had come from Darlington three weeks earlier, as that was the due date, but she was scheduled to leave the next day. As the three of us (or shall I say, four of us) started off to St. Luke's Hospital, an hour's drive through the city, we learned that the snow had begun melting on the streets. With the tire chains breaking and hitting the side of the car, we had to find a filling station to remove them. The attendant charged fifty cents, which I didn't have, so I had to tell him that we were having a baby and I'd come back with the money. He let us go.

The delay became terrifying, and in 1962 there were no such things as cell phones or 911 service. We ran through all the red lights, hoping the police would stop us and escort us, but none did. As we sped through the streets of Kansas City, my mother said from the backseat, "Don't worry, I'm ready." She showed Rose her paper sack filled

Me holding baby Rusty, 1962   *Rusty and me*

with rubber gloves, scissors, and a ball of string. Rusty was born just minutes after arriving at the hospital. [Rose remembers, "Rusty's birth was on the same day astronaut John Glenn circled the Earth for the first time. If Rusty had weighed nine pounds he would have been a hero and received many presents; he weighed eight pounds fifteen ounces!"]

Another family experience was the opportunity to perform the marriage of my own grandmother, Nana. My grandfather, Popie, had died five years earlier. Nana had brought Earl Thompson to our house for us to meet him on the night Rusty was born. They later referred to that night as the "water-breaking party." All the Kansas City Bostons and friends gathered at Northminster for the wedding. Rose and I enjoyed many nights playing cards with Nana and Earl.

A very significant event that had an impact on me and the congregation took place during the construction of the new sanctuary. When the bids were made, the lowest bid was from the Mormon church that was located directly across the street from Northminster. It was an unusual and unexpected bid, significantly lower than the others. The Mormon church and Mormon people usually kept to themselves and were generally regarded as odd religious folks, certainly not the Christian type. After consulting with other churches they had worked with, the decision was made to accept the bid, though many church members were concerned. The construction was completed far ahead of the projected schedule and the architect who had been hired to inspect the construction remarked when it was finished, "You didn't need to hire me. The Mormons' work went above and beyond specification." When the dedication was held, the Mormon congregation joined in on the celebration. For me and our congregation, a new respect developed for the Mormon church and their community.

Life at Northminster was good. The church was growing. We loved our home. Rose was involved with the women in the church. Robin and Rusty enjoyed the children's program. We all enjoyed being a part of the church family, along with the activities of our extended family. Thoughts of returning to the original idea of finding a residential program to become a hospital chaplain had left our minds. Rose and I both entertained the notion that we could retire in Kansas City. Yet it was not to be.

In the fall of 1964, our fourth year at Northminster, I received a letter from James Alexander, the executive director of our denominational department that has oversight over Presbyterian ministers serving out of bounds of their local presbytery, such as hospital and military chaplains, heads of institutions, and missionary work. He stated that due to the military buildup for the war in Vietnam there was a shortage of Presbyterian chaplains on active duty in the U.S. Army. Since I was already a chaplain in the Missouri National Guard, he asked if I would consider going on active duty for three years. He said to give him an answer as soon as possible, but for some reason I could not come up with an answer.

When Rose read the letter, she said she knew what to say and she would type the response for me. Her words to me were, "You are needed right here in Kansas City." Yet I procrastinated for days, which I have always been good at doing. I spent many nights reasoning, pondering, and praying. It certainly would have been easy to stay at Northminster. But I realized there were a number of ministers who would be interested in a church like Northminster, but there would be few eligible to serve on active duty. Rose and I privately discussed the possibilities pro and con for so long that I received a terse letter from James Alexander asking why I had not responded.

In our discussions, the cons were: The Vietnam War could mean a year's separation; the kids were settled in the preschool activities; we liked the church and the church seemed like us; and we liked our home and enjoyed our extended family. On the positive side, I was told that if I volunteered, we would likely be sent to the post we requested, and I would ask for Fort Jackson in Columbia, South Carolina, only seventy miles from Darlington, which would take us closer to our mutual families. Then after three years we could look for a church or a hospital chaplain position near Darlington. As much as we enjoyed being in Kansas City there was always in the back of our minds the hope we could go back to the Southeast.

Finally, we made the second life-changing decision of our married life. We joined the army. I gave Rose a book called *The Army Wife* for Christmas in 1965.

CHAPTER SIXTEEN

ARMY CHAPLAIN

Our tour was to begin January 2, 1966. The army wanted me to go to chaplain school in New York for a month of training in combat readiness. Rose and the children stayed in the manse while I was in school to prepare for the move. The chief of the chaplain's office was unable to contact me at school to inform me of my first assignment, so they called Rose at home and informed her that we would be going to the basic-training center in Fort Ord, California. When I called Rose that evening, she was hysterical. To say she was upset would not describe the moment. Her hurt and anger were directed first at me, then at the U.S. government and chief of chaplains. "You told me...." I was disappointed, too. Instead of going south we were going further west. I was upset also because the office called Rose first instead of me. I would've found a gentler way to tell her when I got home. But it was done.

During our farewell party at the church the congregation let us know that they were going with us in their thoughts and prayers and asked us to keep them informed of our military experience.

On February 5, with our station wagon filled to capacity, Rose, Robin, and Rusty, along with Reeney, our lovable dachshund, headed toward Fort Ord, California with a moving van carrying all our earthly possessions. My cousin Donnie followed us in his convertible Cadillac, "to make sure we got there okay."

The sights and sounds of the Old West were exciting and helped soothe our disappointments, especially our stop at

Chaplain's family

the Grand Canyon. The trip took three days. Our last stop was in Las Vegas, where we said goodbye to Donnie. He went to Los Angeles to visit Aunt Virginia and we went on to Fort Ord. We stayed a week in the Officers' Club, waiting for the moving van to arrive.

Fort Ord sits high in the hills overlooking the Bay of Monterey and the Pacific Ocean beyond. To our surprise there were no weather reports in the newspapers or on TV. In this part of California, the weather ranges from 68° at night to 72° during the day. It rains only between three and five o'clock in the morning. There is no fall, winter, or summer, only spring. We would miss the seasons, but it was good not to worry about the weather. We were no longer so excited about a snowfall.

We lived in a three-bedroom duplex on the base with other military families. I was assigned to the Third Brigade, comprised of some four hundred soldiers along with sergeants and officers. Most of the brigade were young men between the ages of eighteen and twenty-one, who had been drafted to serve in Vietnam. They would be training for six weeks and then shipped overseas. My work was to visit them in the barracks and in the fields and specifically those who were overly stressed—and there were plenty of those, who had left the homes where they grew up to live in a barracks with four hundred other men to prepare for war. Located on the base at a beautiful white stone chapel, we had services on Sundays and prayer meetings on Wednesday nights.

Counseling young men was a new experience for me. In civilian life men of this age normally did not ask for counseling unless they were forced. The most difficult times for me were at the end of the six-week trainings when all the new soldiers together were allowed ninety minutes to visit the chaplain's office to share any mental, emotional, spiritual, or family reason they should not be sent overseas.

Army Family, Fort Ord 1965

Promotion Ceremony

It was my responsibility to determine the seriousness of their requests. When I went to my office in the chapel for this assigned period, I found twenty soldiers lined up at my door. By the clock, I figured I had about six minutes with each to determine the seriousness of their situations. Apart from their stress, I enjoyed and learned a lot working with these young men.

As the months passed, our feelings of disappointment at being sent west instead of back east began to change. On the weekends when we were free we toured the surrounding attractions, such as Pebble Beach and Carmel-by-the-Sea, where the rich and famous lived. We especially enjoyed a drive down Highway 1 by the Pacific Ocean. We enjoyed our visits to Yosemite National Park, San Francisco, and the forests of giant sequoias. We especially enjoyed our family picnics on the rocks bordering the ocean, which was always too cold even to wade in the water.

There was a lot of social life on the base. The Officers' Wives Club had numerous projects and activities. There was a farewell party almost every week for a commander who was being assigned to another post. I wore my formal blue uniform and Rose put on her formal gown. These were storybook occasions that we had never experienced. We played bridge with our neighbor next door; we men took the game seriously, while the women had more fun. Robin was in her first year of kindergarten and Rusty went to a Little Folks School located on the base. In addition, there was a beautiful golf course on the base, where I played once or twice a week.

After six months, I was promoted to captain and sent for a month of training at a noted institute for marriage and family counseling in Hollywood. During the evening, a group of us chaplains visited some of the famous restaurants, like The Captain's Tables, where Hollywood stars ate. We ordered either a dessert or a salad because we could not afford a full meal. Our time was spent staring at those actors and actresses we recognized.

All in all, it was an adventurous year for our family. But there was another life change about to happen. Upon returning from a Thanksgiving trip to Yosemite National Park we found an official-looking note on our front door asking me to report to the office of my brigade commander on Monday morning. At that meeting, I was informed that I was being reassigned to the Twelfth Evac Hospital, which was being assembled there at Fort Ord and scheduled to be shipped to Vietnam in March 1966. It looked like I was going to be a hospital chaplain after all, which I had planned to be while in seminary. Rose and the children would move back home to Darlington.

Captain Chaplain Boston

CHAPTER SEVENTEEN

THE TWELFTH EVAC HOSPITAL

My new assignment would be quite a change, from being the chaplain for four hundred young men in basic training to serving the patients and staff of a fifty-six-bed hospital that was similar to the hospital in the TV serial *M*A*S*H*. When I reported to the hospital, which was on the other side of Fort Ord, there were only two staff members, myself and a staff sergeant, who had been assigned to watch over all the hospital equipment that had been stored in a warehouse for over a year. The personnel at the hospital were scheduled to arrive during the months of January and February. The staff would include sixteen physicians, sixteen nurses, approximately forty medical technicians, and a chaplain. My initial responsibility was to greet each person as they arrived and orient them to their temporary living conditions while awaiting shipment March 1 to Vietnam. Rose, Robin, and Rusty remained at Fort Ord until two weeks before the hospital was shipped out.

Most of the hospital staff would come from San Antonio, Texas, where most medical personnel are trained for war-like conditions. Most came by air through San Francisco International Airport. As you might imagine, all who arrived were in some form of semi-shock, including myself. The majority of the physicians and nurses had been drafted out of their private practices and sent to San Antonio, leaving their families behind, similar to the young draftees living in the barracks. This presented a therapeutic situation that I had never experienced or learned about in any classes. I could not find any literature on the subject.

To use an old expression, "I had to learn by the seat of my Army fatigues." It was the emotionally ill leading the emotionally ill and the worst was yet to come. The toughest part was waiting for the departure with nothing to do but sightsee. At least I still had my family and golf clubs with me. It was a depressing and heart-wrenching situation, counting the days until March 1.

Two weeks before March 1 the commanding officer at the hospital received an order from the U.S. Surgeon General's office that the departure of the Twelfth Evac Hospital had been deferred until further notice. This created more anxiety and depression, especially for those who were separated from their families. Since it was two weeks before the initial departure, the moving van had already picked up our furniture and was headed to Darlington. The moving company notified the driver and our furniture was brought back the same day. Not knowing how long "Until further notice" would last, most of those whose families were not already at Fort Ord moved their families to California at their own expense. Six months later a new date was set. August 1 sounded final.

Three weeks before the moving company picked up our furniture again, the Boston family toured cross country back to Darlington, South Carolina. We visited interesting sites, but no one seemed very interested. Melancholia seemed to pervade the whole family, knowing that in two weeks I would be leaving for at least a year in a war-torn country. I had taken three weeks leave to enjoy the family back in Darlington but there was little enjoyment. I wished I had taken only a few days before leaving, just to help the family move back. We had rented a home next door to my mother and dad, which gave me some relief.

On July 28 I boarded an Air Force C141 bound for the Oakland, California naval base with Rose, Robin, Rusty, and our beloved Reeney standing outside the terminal waving. Tears flowed down my face. I did not want to look back, but just before entering the door, at the top of the ramp, I did, and wondered, "Will I ever see them again?"

When I arrived in Oakland, I rented a hotel room, since I could not board the ship, the U.S.S. *Patrick*, until the next day. My anxieties kept me awake most of the night but at least I was safe. The next morning, I took a taxi to board the ship. We were expected to set sail at 1600 (4 p.m.). I did not board the ship right away, because I was told that once we were on board we could not get off and I wanted to make more phone calls back home. I roamed around the docks going from one pay phone booth to another because there were a lot of sailors waiting to call. If you made more than one call you got some ugly catcalls. I called as many of the family in Darlington and Kansas City as I could afford. I knew that once I went on board I would only be able to communicate by letters for the next year or more.

At 1400 I went aboard. My official orders said to be aboard at 1200 (noon). I relied on my chaplain's bars for an excuse when I was met and welcomed by a navy chaplain who took me to a private stateroom that had been reserved for me. I was glad to have a room of my own. I was tired of putting on my brave minister's face. I closed the doors, sat down on the bed, and cried.

At exactly 1600 the ship's horn began to sound, the engines began to rumble, my throat clogged, and my heart skipped a beat. We were underway. After a few minutes, I thought it was time to join the troops. I put my ministerial face back on and went up on deck. Many of the hospital staff were standing on the side taking in the scenery of the San Francisco Bay. Straight ahead was the Golden Gate Bridge. I had seen many pictures of the bridge, but never in person and now I was going under it instead of over it. But just before going under it the ship began to turn around and headed back to shore. There was a loud chatter expressing the thoughts that maybe the hospital had been deferred again. As the ship turned, it circled the Alcatraz prison, and then headed back out to sea. The next stop would be the Philippines.

We were issued tablets if needed for seasickness. I did not miss a day taking mine. About four or five days later we docked at the port of Manila and were given twenty-four hours to go ashore. I stayed on the ship. There was in the back of my mind, and I suspect in most of the minds aboard, the hope and wish that the war would suddenly end, and we would be taken back to Fort Ord. But it was not to be.

Three days later we docked at Vũng Tàu, Vietnam. The trip was uneventful except for an unannounced ceremony. The staff at the hospital were told that this was a two-hundred-year tradition, that any serviceman or woman crossing the equator aboard a ship for the first time must be initiated. The initiation involved being stripped naked except for your shorts (some took those off, too) to be covered with shaving cream and hosed off after passing the equator. I thought of using my cross and captain bars to be excused but decided to go with the crowd. It turned out to be fun and I had my first laugh in seven days. I had put aside my dignity and my ministerial look and became a real human being.

For security reasons the hospital equipment and staff were put on barges at night. My first sight of the country was a sky lit up with flares. It rocked to the sounds of guns, mortars, bombs, and jet fighter planes overhead. The next day we boarded army trucks and were taken to the city of Biên Hòa, sixty miles inland. Four large tents had been set up for temporary housing; that was to become our home for the next three months. This delay was due to a military and political mix-up. The hospital had not been built.

CHAPTER EIGHTEEN

My Vietnam Story

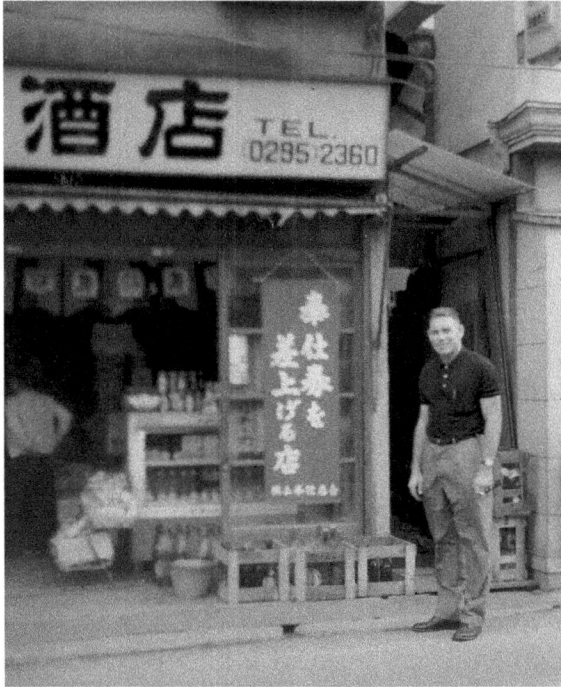

Vietnam tourist

My first place to call home in Vietnam was an army-is-sued canvas cot against the wall of a forty-man tent. The bathroom lavatory, called "the head," looked like a horse stable. In each stable was a sink, shower, and a five-hundred-gallon barrel overhead. The latrine was in back of the stable. It looked and smelled like a farmer's outhouse stretched to accommodate ten servicemen at a time. When I first saw it, I thought to myself, I'm used to privacy, I'll bet I'll be constipated most of my tour. The chow hall was about a five-minute walk away. The food was good.

I was told by the hospital commander, who was a surgeon, that, since the hospital would not be ready for patients until after Thanksgiving, I would be free to tour the country and visit other hospitals. He strongly suggested that we use helicopters, not Jeeps or army trucks, when possible. My first inclination was to find a secure foxhole, and put up a sign that read, "Chaplain on call." The physicians were given the choice to help assemble the hospital or visit other hospitals where needed; most chose to help with the construction.

After a couple of days I got up my nerve and hopped a flight to Saigon and visited the field hospital, the mother of all military hospitals in the country. I enjoyed meeting the chaplains and most of all I enjoyed finding a private restroom to do my business. I inquired at the Vietnam command center if there was a unit that needed a chaplain to fill in and was told that all the positions were filled at the present time. I took a flight back to the base in Biên Hòa and spent most of my waking time mingling with the troops and those Vietnamese citizens who spoke English. I thought of myself as the wandering chaplain. I remember thinking, "How did I get myself so misplaced, so far from home and family?"

Within those first few weeks an infection developed on my rear end that made it difficult for me to sit down. I went to one of the doctors for an examination. He told me I had what is called a pilonidal cyst, and that it needed surgery to be removed or it would get worse in the hot climate. Since my assignment at the hospital would not start until after Thanksgiving, arrangements were made to send me to a military hospital in Japan, since there were no medical facilities in Vietnam that were equipped to handle this kind of surgery. I felt a tinge of guilt boarding a C-141 transport loaded with soldiers with wounds so bad they had to be sent home.

I was in Japan for three weeks. After the first week, I was put on convalescent leave and took the opportunity to tour the country. One of the technicians at our hospital in Vietnam was married to a Japanese girl who was living with her family in Tokyo. He asked if I would visit her family while I was there. I did and had a wonderful experience with three generations living together over a shop where everyone worked. I was invited to have dinner with the family, which was both an awkward and delightful experience.

The awkwardness came from the custom that when the family came to eat the oldest male, referred to as Papasan, would be served his plate and start eating before the other men in the family joined him. Added to that custom was another that when there was a male visitor, he was expected to take the place of Papasan and begin eating first. The female members were allowed to eat only after the male members finished their meal and after dinner conversation. We sat on the floor around a large table with a hibachi grill in the middle filled with sizzling steak. There I sat with chopsticks in one hand and a fork provided by the wife of my friend, not knowing what to do next. I wanted everyone to join me before I began eating. Realizing their custom came before my wish, I figured it out with a little guidance and laughter and had a delightful experience. The next day the soldier's wife took me on a tour around Tokyo.

I found the citizens of Japan, young and old, to be very friendly and hospitable. On one excursion I took a couple of days to tour Mount Fuji, the tallest mountain in Japan. When the train stopped at one of the villages, I went to find a motel. To my surprise I could not find a person who could speak English. I managed to gesture enough to rent a room for the night. It was not dark, so I decided to shop around the village. In a short time, I began to notice that someone was following me. It felt creepy, but I found out later that when someone who does not speak Japanese checks into a hotel, someone is paid to follow him or her inconspicuously in case he gets lost.

When I was dismissed from the hospital, I was given a room to stay in until word was received from Vietnam that our hospital was ready to receive patients. During this time, I was asked to visit those who had been wounded in Vietnam and were waiting to be able to return to the states.

Sometime around the middle of November I received word that the hospital in Vietnam was almost complete and would soon begin receiving patients. I had been holding a secret hope that the command in Vietnam would change my orders to continue my work at the hospital in Japan, but my hope did not come true. The hospital was located near a small village named C☐ Chi. This also was the base of the Army Twenty-fifth Division. The base was approximately one square mile, surrounded by rolls and rolls of barb wire. One day after I arrived, sixteen nurses arrived by helicopters. We took our first patients on December 13, 1966.

The most difficult and heart-wrenching duty I had as the chaplain of an evac hospital in a war zone was my triage assignment. Whenever there was a fire fight within reach of the hospital, a medivac helicopter brought in the wounded. Usually there were from sixteen to thirty men who needed immediate medical attention. In order to provide medical services to the most men, those whose wounds were the most critical and would require more intensive treatment were carried to a Quonset hut just outside the emergency room. Each was given a shot for pain and his treatment was delayed. Some conditions were fatal.

My assignment was to visit each soldier waiting for treatment and provide some kind of hope and encouragement, knowing that some would not make it for treatment. Nothing had prepared me for this kind of situation. Each man was brought in on a stretcher and laid on the side of

Army man

the hut. Some were conscious, some were not. The only thing I could think to do was to lean down on one knee, hold each man by his hand, and ask him to repeat after me the Lord's Prayer. Some did, some did not. This scene took place numerous times in the years 1966-67.

Now fast forward ten to fifteen years. On one given Sunday, after dinner, I received a strange phone call from an unknown source. It began this way: "Is your name Robert W. Boston?" I hesitantly said, "Yes, it is." Then he asked, "Is there a possibility that you served as a chaplain in the U.S. Army in Vietnam in 1967?" I responded, "Yes, I was there." Suddenly the phone became silent. After I said "Hello? Hello?" several times, the voice came back. A man told me he had been searching for a chaplain named Boston for a number of years at army bases and directories across the country. There was a moment of silence and I could sense an emotional breakdown on his part. He then told me his story.

This young man had been lying scared and hurt the night he was brought to the hospital. He remembered looking up and seeing someone kneeling down, holding his hand, and repeating the Lord's Prayer with him. He had remembered seeing a silver cross and the name "Boston" just below. After that all he could remember was being flown out to the army hospital in Japan and then several weeks later to the Walter Reed Hospital in the U.S. for several months. He was now living with his wife and two children in California. He wanted me to know that when he discovered where he was, he continued to repeat the Lord's Prayer. When he got married, the Lord's Prayer was sung at his wedding and at the baptism of his children. It is repeated every Sunday when the family gathers for dinner. By this time in his story I was emotionally drained. We talked for a while, took each other's phone number and said we wanted to stay in touch. He did not call again. I did not call, and I regret that.

My life and work for the next eight months are best described by the letters I sent home to family, friends, and my friends back at Northminster Presbyterian Church.

LETTERS FROM VIETNAM, 1966-1967

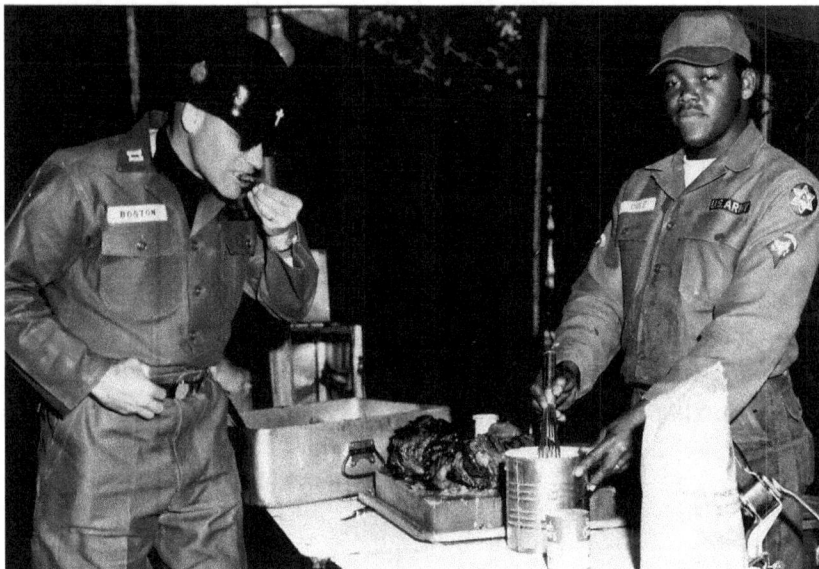

Chaplain Boston

October 1966

To Our Friends at Northminster....

Much has happened. Many miles have passed and sailed by since that family night in July. It meant so much to Rose and me to visit Northminster and to see so many of you again....

My first impression of life in Vietnam is indescribable. You have to see it to believe and understand it. The first couple of days I experienced a mixture of fright, loneliness, depression, and pity. In the distant woods and fields, you see and hear constantly the explosion of bombs, mortars, and guns, and wonder if they might come your way. You lie awake at night staring at the top of a tent—your mind wanders back and forth—to the family back home, haunted with the fear of never seeing them again—to the faces you have seen over here, bewildered and hungry men, women, and little children standing by the road watching army trucks go by—to a comfortable suburban parish back in the States—to the blast of a mortar and a roar of a jet overhead and in the hills beyond—to trout fishing at Bennett Springs—to the hard cot under your body. Somehow you begin to adjust and live with it.

I have asked the question—do we need to be here fighting this war? Do the Vietnamese want us? Are we wasting human lives for nothing? For an answer I have gone to the wounded here in the hospital—those whose battered and torn bodies and exhausted minds tell of their risks and sacrifices—those who have given the most for the cause. Almost without exception both officers and enlisted men express the conviction that this war is a must—the people of South Vietnam, for the most part, do want us because they know what the alternative is like. Somehow the views of these men who have given so much seems more valid than those expressed in some social and church circles back in the States.

I have asked also what my mission as a minister to these men is. Life here is not the same as I knew it back in America. There, a man's problem usually relates in some way to his job or his family. Over here he has no family. Probably he went to school to be an accountant, etc., but here his job may be to clean out a latrine or destroy a certain village.

The chaplain talks about faith, hope, and love, God's care, prayer. The soldier knows a boy who prayed often and was killed. He knows another guy who never prayed and he went back home without a scratch. The chaplain talks about eternal life. The only eternity most think of is that which comes at the end of a twelve-month tour. What can you say to these men who are living an existence so unnatural, so unreal? I am searching for answers! It is the greatest challenge of my ministry so far. I covet your prayers.

God be with you till we meet again—

Chaplain Robert W. Boston

Cu Chi, Vietnam

13 December 1966
Our Dear Friends and Relatives,

As this Christmas approaches, I have mixed emotions. In a way I look forward to Christmas in Vietnam: the singing of the carols to the music of a tiny field organ and a couple of banjos; a lull in the fighting on Christmas Day and New Year's; two days of peace; two nights of sleep without the sound of guns and bombs; communion on Christmas morning; the Bob Hope show; distributing gifts and care packages to a homeless bunch of guys; sharing the goodies, cards, letters, and hope from home. This will be the most memorable Christmas of my life, past or future.

But in another way, it will be the most difficult ever. For purely selfish reasons, I want to be home for Christmas. The thought of being away from my family is already beginning to haunt me. My adjustment to the weather in these primitive and dangerous living conditions has been much easier than I imagined. But the pain of separation from those three people in South Carolina is still with me. I am afraid this will be my "thorn in the flesh" for as long as I am here.

Christmas in a war zone is quite different from any place in the world. In many ways, it comes closer to being what Christmas should be. Over here there is no commercialization, no manger scenes or Santa Clauses enticing us to come and buy something. Over here the thoughts and cares behind the packages received outweigh 1,000 times the gifts in them. Over here Christmas is not just for children but is a day of peace and memories and hope for every man and woman. Over here a simple Christmas tree will warm the hearts of hundreds of men. Not one will wither on a vacant lot. Over here there will be no shut-ins to cheer up, for, in a real sense, everyone is shut-in. Over here singing carols on Christmas Day and receiving Holy Communion on Christmas morning will have for most people a far deeper meaning than ever before. Over here Christmas is a feeling: a mixture of war and peace, hopes and dreams, remembrances and trying to forget. Over here, "Peace on Earth and Goodwill toward Men" is more than a message printed on a card.

Our hospital is located on an army post near the village of Cu Chi, about 35 miles northwest of Saigon. The area surrounding the post is infested with elements of the Viet Cong. It would be good if we could share a little of the true Christmas with the natives around us in this part of the country. It is impossible to discern between friend and enemy. We want to help them both, but we also want to be here next Christmas.

This is the ugliest and most controversial war our country has ever fought, yet I have become convinced not as an army officer but as a minister and still a civilian at heart that it is necessary and worth the price being paid. History in general and America in particular has never set a price on freedom, for itself or for others. Another Christmas will strengthen even more this dedication.

Until recently, we have been unable to have a full religious program because the hospital has been in the construction stage. My duties have been limited to one worship service on Sunday morning, and some personal counseling among the hospital personnel. But now that the major construction is completed and patients are being received, activity is increasing. Last week we organized a choir made up of nurses, doctors, and medical officers and corpsmen. So far there are 15 voices and interest is expected to increase. They will sing at all of our worship services and when invited will provide entertainment and music for other units on special occasions. On Christmas Eve, the choir will go out in ambulances to combat units to sing Christmas carols. They will be a big hit for female voices in a war zone are a rare and welcomed commodity.

Our place of worship on Sunday morning is unique in itself. The services are being conducted temporarily in the Cu Chi A-Go-Go, or what is popularly known as the beer tent. On Saturday night the air rings with "He's a Jolly Good Fellow" to the background of clanging cans, poker chips, and the best of army jokes. Then a few hours later the same crowd gathers a little more somber to the tune of "Holy, Holy, Holy," accompanied by the finest organ music and sincerest voices ever heard. Plans are underway to build a little chapel on the hospital site, which will add much to our worship, but then take a little something away from the experience we are now having. The army is unable to provide a chapel for each unit here, but our people seem to be intent upon having a chapel of their own. It will take time. The men will have to finance it and build it themselves in their free time, with material that has to be borrowed, scrounged, and purchased here, there, and wherever. It will not be easy but who wants a church that comes easy? I had at one time thought that at least with this congregation, I won't be bothered with a building fund program. But it has not worked out quite that way.

Already I have received a number of cards and packages from you. Each one will mean far more this Christmas than any in the past. The enjoyment of the goodies will multiply for I will share them with as many as I can and still keep some for selfish purposes.

Rose, Robin, and Rusty are doing fine in Darlington. They are enjoying for the first time grandparents to spoil them. Rose has done so well in running a home, raising and educating the children, managing all the repairs, finances, and problems a husband and father normally handles, which is no surprise to anyone who knows her. According to her first report card, Robin is enjoying and doing so good in her first year of school. She has all her teeth back, sings in the children's choir at church, and is slowly becoming a young lady. Rusty still cannot pronounce his R's but pronounces everything else. He is going to preschool, has lost his baby plumpness, keeps all the old folks agile with his ball playing. Both kids are keeping Rose hopping. All are a little frustrated without me. At least I like to think that.

They all join me in wishing you and yours the happiest and most meaningful holiday season ever.

"God be with you till we meet again".

Bob, And in Spirit, Rose, Robin, Rusty

April 20, 1967

My Dear Friends and Relatives,

You have been so kind and good to write and I have been able to do so little in return. As a way of letting you know how I feel about you and receiving your letters, cards, boxes of goodies, and encouragements, I write this letter. If I could, I would write every one of you separately and often. I will try to answer the questions you have asked and share with you some of the experiences that I have had during the past two months.

When I wrote you last Christmas our hospital was yet to receive its first battle casualty. Since that letter 2,231 have been admitted through the emergency room. 1,223 of these boys have been returned to the rice paddies and jungles; 714 were evacuated to Japan or back to the States; 57 didn't make it to either place. Behind and beyond every one of these boys there is a story to be told. Some very heartwarming and thrilling … some tragic and sickening. I talked and listened with each man. Most of their names are forgotten, but their experiences, their longings and anxieties, hopes and fears will be with me from that day on.

Let me share with you one day at the hospital here in Cu Chi. A typical one begins around 7:30. Breakfast normally consists of a can of juice, grapefruit or peaches, along with the piece of whatsoever kind of goodies is left in the box from home. At 8:30 I normally begin my rounds starting with the intensive care wards. These are the boys who are the more seriously wounded, with head and chest wounds, burns and amputees.

Those in these wards fall into two general categories: those who will eventually return to duty as their wounds will heal in a matter of weeks or a couple of months and

those who will be
returning to the
States because of
permanent injury
or wounds that will
take many months
to heal. Each kind
has its own fears
and frustrations.
For those returning
home there is the joy
of knowing they will
not be returning to
the hell and anguish
they have known.
Yet many are fear-

Vietnam Monkey

ful of their readjustments to civilian life and whether
they will be accepted with a scarred face, an artificial leg
or arm. With these men, I try to help them through their
first major obstacle, not to feel sorry for themselves, nor
to allow anyone else to do so. As to the other group, their
physical wounds are less serious but their anxieties are
even greater. They must return to the very same horrors
in danger they never thought they would live through
once, much less twice or possibly a third time. With these
men, I have no instant prescription of courage and faith,
only sympathy and time to listen to their thoughts and
feelings.

From here I go to the convalescent wards where the
problems are much the same but usually less severe. I
pass by the bed of each man. Depending upon the individual's needs in response, I may sit on the side of a bed
for a few minutes, sometimes an hour. We talk about the
war, a particular battle, a buddy who didn't make it, a
girlfriend, a wife who hasn't been faithful, a letter that
needs to be written, what it means and feels like to take

the life of another human being, a mother and father who haven't been notified because "they would worry too much," what they plan to do when their tour is over, is this war worth the price being paid?, what is God doing about all this confusion of humanity, whose side is He on? Sometimes we pray together. Most of the time I just listen and try to understand.

At any time during my rounds, a call may come from the emergency room that a helicopter is five minutes out bringing three liters and an ambulatory patient. I rush over to the chopper pad with a couple of nurses, a doctor, two liter bearers. We wait and watch for the bird with a Red Cross on its nose, better known as "dust-off." He lands. We wait anxiously to see how much life is there. They are carried into the emergency room, placed on two sawhorses underneath bottles that can very quickly be filled with blood plasma and glucose. The hectic and dedicated attempt to save a life begins. My task is to give what assurance and comfort I can. Sometimes a boy will release a cross or medal around his neck and grasp my hand. I try to tell him in so many words, "I know that your pain is great, but you are going to be alright." Some appear calm and assured. Some show no outward response. I have not always told the truth. Most make it back, but a few don't. This bit of drama is repeated at unpredicted intervals throughout the day and night.

By 3:00 PM, I have usually managed to see every patient. For the next few hours prior to supper I may write a few letters, read one of the last months' Time magazines, think about a sermon for Sunday, daydream about Rose, Robin, and Rusty. After supper, my activities vary from night to night. One out of 20 there is a good movie shown on an outdoor screen, where everybody brings their own chairs. I may drop by the enlisted men's barracks, wander through the beer tent, go back to see a critically ill patient, join a bull session with the doctors, play chess or bridge. This is my day. It may vary some but very little during the seven days of the week.

In the last month a little excitement has been added, Viet Cong mortar attacks. The first one came in March. We have had five more since. Fortunately, no one here in the hospital has been hit but we have spent some sleepless nights. They come anytime between dusk and dawn. They last from 10 minutes to several hours. They give no warning. When an explosion happens where it is not supposed to, everyone that is awake shouts "Mortar!" and there is a mad scramble to a sandbagged bunker next to the tent. There we sit and wait and utter silent prayers. When "All Clear" is sounded we hurry to the emergency room knowing there will soon be a number of casualties from throughout the base camp. As we work with these wounded there is the added painful realization, "That could well have been one of us."

So goes 24 hours a day. Add to this 100-130-degree weather, land that is either too dusty or too wet, the constant sounds of cannon fire going the other way and bombings, outdoor toilets and showers, no wife and children, and you don't have too much to be joyful about, but there is a sense of appreciation developed and an experience in human suffering that no seminary or parish in the world could ever offer.

I have had the opportunity to do some traveling, exclusively by helicopter. I have been in most major cities and towns, a few hamlets and outposts in this part of Vietnam. From each place, the war looks different. This is not one war but many wars with many fronts, each requiring a strategy all of its own.

You have probably heard many stories about the bar girls, prostitutes' hotels, brothels, and the American soldier. Regrettably most of them are true. I did not want

Vietnam bunker

to believe it either but I could not keep my eyes shut. This is not so much a reflection on an individual background and training as it is the inhuman circumstances these boys live under. The medics caution the boys on the dangers involved. The chaplains caution the boys by encouraging them to stay away. The medics usually have the largest congregation.

I haven't learned the language but have used every opportunity to observe and study the culture, traditions, and peculiarities of the Vietnamese people. I have tried to discover their honest feelings about having American troops in their country. This is difficult because it is a trait of the Oriental people to tell a stranger what they think he wants to hear rather than the truth. But from their actions you can sense that like Americans back home, they too are divided and confused. Some want us here because they have experienced the exploits of Communism. Others want us here because they are getting rich off of the American soldiers' money. Still others are extremely hostile over our presence here, because they have seen and witnessed their women, land, and cities raped by our army and its arsenal of weapons. Then there are many who just want to be left alone to grow their rice, live quietly in their homes, and raise their children. I have taken hundreds of slides, mostly of civilian life.

I wish I could give you an optimistic view on the prospects for peace over here. But from where I am, the end is not in sight. It has become politically fashionable to propose a "peace plan." Each attempt in the past brought a spark of hope, but most now have become numb to all such talk. Only God knows where the answer lies and He must be somewhat confused and irritated over the behavior of both sides.

Sunday in Vietnam is very much like any other day. It may be punctuated by a worship service at 1000 hours, if there are not too many casualties being flown in at that hour, otherwise everything goes on much like the Saturday before and the Monday after. It is necessary on Saturday afternoon to remind both patients and hospital personnel that tomorrow is Sunday. On several occasions, I have had to remind myself. The chapel I told you about in my Christmas letter is nearly complete and a dedication service will be held on 28 May. When finished it will be bought and paid for by contributions of hospital personnel and patients.

Our next project is to start a clothes closet at the hospital to be used by Vietnamese civilians. We receive every week from 10-20 men, women, and children who have been caught in the crossfire of our bombs, artillery, mortars, and those of the Viet Cong. Many of these people have lost everything they owned. It would be good to be able to give them at least a change of clothes as they return to their homes, which in some cases have been destroyed. You want so much to offer them some spiritual help, but the language barrier makes this impossible. A tangible gift could say more than words.

That is the story from this end of the world. With a little more than three months to go (102 days), I can truthfully say I am glad I came, and I am glad that I am coming home.

Love, Bob

Touring Vietnam

CHAPTER TWENTY

COMING HOME, GETTING LOST

Home from Vietnam, Darlington, 1967

On August 31, 1967 my duffel bag and I departed the airbase at Biên Hòa (the place I first called home in Vietnam) on a 747 Pan Am jet with two hundred other GIs. Our personal wars were not over yet. Looking out the window we could still see mortars exploding near the runway. As the plane sped down the runway and began its climb, there was a dead silence throughout the plane. Then in a few minutes, which felt like an hour, a voice came through the cabin, "This is your captain. We are at 10,000 feet. Welcome to America." The plane exploded with tears of relief, joy, and celebration.

The flight from Vietnam to Oakland, California and on to Atlanta, Georgia went without a hitch. Then while waiting

Darlington Homecoming

on the runway in Atlanta, only twenty-five minutes from home, the captain announced that the airport in Charleston was closed due to fog. Delta had arranged to have a limousine take the passengers on to Charleston, where my family was waiting for me. Finally, after six hours of delay, the moment I had been longing for the past 365 days arrived and the hugs and tears began to flow at the fogged-in Charleston airport.

My next assignment was the basic-training center at Fort Jackson South Carolina, the place I had requested three years before.

Upon my return, one of the first trips I wanted to plan was to go trout fishing in the mountains of North Carolina. When I was in Kansas City, I had learned the art of trout fishing and had fished at Bennett Springs, Missouri every spring and fall. Carl Metzger, my brother-in-law who lived in Easley, South Carolina, told me that his back-door neighbor was an excellent trout man and had knowledge of all the best streams in North Carolina, and was willing to go with us. We set a date, February 8, 1968. I remember it vividly. It was on a Saturday. For reasons I cannot remember the neighbor was unable to go, but he drew a detailed map for where to put in on the Chattooga River, a rough and fast stream, which later became the scene of the movie *Deliverance*.

We left Easley at daylight on Saturday, equipped with our fly fishing rods, an assortment of flies, light jackets, and our detailed map of where to park the car and walk to the river. The weather forecast was perfect for a day of fishing. The temperature was predicted to be in the mid-sixties. Our plans were to walk the stream until about four o'clock, and then walk back to the car, which was approximately two miles from the river.

We found the parking area, which was beside the main highway. After putting on our waders and fishing jackets, supplied with a couple of sandwiches and a cold drink, we followed the map to a well-worn mountain trail directly across the highway from the parking area.

According to the map the river was about an hour's walk away. After walking for over an hour we came to a fork in the trail which was not on the map. After studying the two trails we decided to go on the left one since it was more worn than the one to the right. After another hour or so we began hearing the sound of the roaring Chattooga. I was excited. Carl was his quiet, accommodating self. Once we got to the river, he acknowledged that he did not know much about trout fishing but had been several times just to be with friends. I shared with him what little I remembered about fishing upstream. By this time, it was almost 12 o'clock and we had yet to step in the water. A quick study of the map revealed that if we did not stay in one place too long, in two to three hours we should reach Burrells Ford, a camping site that had a graveled road which would lead back to our car.

We stepped into the water and made our first cast upstream. I began to wonder about the wisdom of fishing and walking upstream rather than going downstream, but that was not what the map by Carl's back-door neighbor indicated. After walking and jumping from one rock to the next and trying to catch a trout in between, it did not take long before two amateurs who had not been fishing for some time grew exhausted. When I realized it was three o'clock, I said to Carl that we were at a point in time that if we turned back now, we could reach our car before dark. After a meeting of minds, we both concluded that Burrells Ford could not be far, according to the map. So, we climbed and fished on.

It did not take long before our anxiety began to get hold of us, and we decided to stop fishing and move upstream as fast as our legs would take us. As the clouds began to roll in, the winds brought a sudden chill, and we knew that darkness would soon follow. We threw away our fishing rods and made canes from hanging tree limbs that helped us move faster. Unfortunately, faster was not fast enough. As the darkness overwhelmed us, we both knew that moving on would risk a broken leg on a slick rock. The underbrush kept us from finding a way out for a time until suddenly there appeared what looked like white sand on the shore. I don't know who saw it first, but we both stumbled toward it. As we walked ashore, we discovered that it was snow left over from the night before.

Immediately, and without speaking, we both knew we had to get a fire started. We began crawling on our hands and knees into the trees and underbrush to find enough dry wood to build a fire. After gathering what we thought to be enough to build a fire the next task was to find a way to start a fire. Neither Carl nor I was adept at starting a fire by rubbing two sticks together. At this moment we experienced two little miracles that may have made a difference in our survival.

Carl searched his pockets and came up with a paper sack in which he had carried some jellybeans. Since I smoked, I had a Zippo lighter in the top pocket of my waders. Carl put his bag under the wood, and I took out my lighter, but as I zipped and zipped, I discovered my lighter was out of fluid. Feeling somewhat desperate, I began searching my pockets, perhaps for a stray match. Astonished, I discovered another Zippo lighter! I had never before carried two lighters at the same time! I usually filled both with fluid and left one at home until the other gave out. I zipped, and the fire started.

The feeling of relief was filled with gratitude and love to our heavenly father, each other, and our families. At this time, we shared our concern for what Bobbie and Rose were going through. They were expecting us for supper.

We spent the rest of the night rolling over and over as close to the fire as we could without catching it and crawling into the trees for more wood and back to the fire before we froze. Carl chuckled and said, "Wonder what would be worse, freezing to death or burning?"

As soon as we saw the light of a new day, we splashed water to put out the fire, picked up our walking sticks, and continued walking upstream on the edge of the river. After walking for about thirty minutes or so we came upon a well-worn hiking path and within the hour we found

Burrells Ford and the gravel road that led up the mountain to the main highway where our car was parked. We both expressed exuberance but at the same moment worried about Bobbie and Rose. They must have also stayed awake all night worrying about what had happened to us. We did not know how far we had to walk but we moved at a fast pace.

Very soon we saw a pickup truck coming down the road. We waved our arms excitedly. When the driver stopped, we told him we had been lost on the river all night and asked him if he would mind taking us up to the main highway where our car was parked. He politely told us, "I'm sorry, gentlemen, but Sunday is the only day I can come fishing. I'm sure somebody else will come by." We then asked him how far the highway was, and he told us, "Maybe a mile or two."

It was another hour or so before we reached the main road. We could see the parking areas and started walking even faster. It was then that we heard someone shout, "There they are!" Someone came in a Jeep to pick us up. But since we had only about fifty yards to go, we declined the ride and made it to the car on our own, only to be greeted by a large group made up of rescue squads from several towns, including Walhalla and Seneca. Part of the group had arrived at dark and waited until morning to begin their search. A breakfast was being prepared for everyone there and they invited us to eat. We declined and said we needed to get back to our families.

As we drove back down the mountain, Carl turned on the radio. During a morning news report, we heard, "A prominent Easley businessman and chaplain from Fort Jackson, South Carolina were thought to be lost on the Chattooga River and rescue units have been called in to the search." We chuckled. I remember breaking down in tears. Carl concentrated on the road and drove on. We heard later that a helicopter from Fort Jackson was to be sent if we were not found by mid-day. It was another emotional moment when we arrived home and hugged our wives and family.

On the River

CHAPTER TWENTY-ONE

LEAVING THE ARMY

Reverend Robert W. Boston

A new and critical life-decision time was upon us again. I had eight months left in my three-year assignment with the U.S. Army. I was offered the opportunity to re-enlist and stay in the army, which offered opportunities for travel, new experiences, with good medical and financial support for the family. There would also be numerous opportunities for church work in civilian life, which we had enjoyed at Northminster Church. There was also a chance for a resident program in hospital chaplaincy that I had wanted when we finished seminary. Rose, as the good wife, said she would go along with whatever I decided. We had a few months to decide so I put the decision aside as I began my work at Fort Jackson's basic-training center, doing the same work I had done at Fort Ord, but this time with a lot more confidence and experience, having already been where most of these young men were going after six weeks of training. There was also the benefit of being close to our families, all of whom were in Darlington.

It was at this time that we experienced the first death in our family. My father died on October 8, 1967, of scoliosis of the liver. He was only fifty-four years old. In many ways this was a relief for my mother, who had endured the emotional, financial, and medical conditions of his drinking problems.

My grief was compounded by the influence he had in my life. Shortly before I went to Vietnam I wrote him a letter that said, "Through the years, Mom, Ronnie, Joy, and I have given you a hard time for your drinking habits and what it was doing to you and the family. But there is another side I could not find the right time or words to tell you about until now. Mom was always there for me at home, school, and ball games, but you taught me more about living in the outside world. You taught me to accept every person just as they are." I reminded him of the story about bringing a German prisoner home for dinner and saying he was just like us. And of his removing the "Colored" sign from the gas station he ran. And telling me, "There is enough good in the best of us and enough bad in the worst of us, that it behooves any of us not to criticize another." I even wrote a sermon about that message. And I explained that he had helped teach me responsibility when he let me have a paper route when Mother had said I was too young. "I have learned that you had an illness you could not conquer," I ended the letter, "but I have never doubted your pride and love for me and the rest of the family. All these things have served me well in my life work and they have been passed down to Robin and Rusty."

The spring of 1968 was upon us, and we still had not made a decision. I was learning that the hardest decisions in life are those between two or more good things when you can only have one.

Then a call came like a "Voice from Heaven." The Southeastern Conference minister of the Presbyterian Church (U.S.A.) called and asked if I would meet with him to discuss a new church development opportunity. It sounded interesting, so we met at a restaurant in Columbia. The new development was the organization of several new United Presbyterian churches in South Carolina and Georgia. There were a number of churches in North Carolina, but the only churches in South Carolina were in the African American community. The Board of National Missions was aware that many members who were moving to southern states were not attending the denomination's churches because of their views regarding segregation and ultra-conservative positions in theology and policy, even though both used the same Book of Church Order. The board had chosen three cities to develop new churches, Columbia, Charleston, and Atlanta. The offer was a salary and housing allotment for five years, including an escrow for land and a suitable church building. In addition, I would have the choice of which city we would like to move to.

After discussing this offer with Rose, we both agreed to accept. The choice of which city was another of those major decisions that would alter the lives of Robin, who was going into the second grade, and Rusty, going to kindergarten, as well as Rose and myself. We chose Charleston. We'd already lived in Columbia and Atlanta, and we'd both heard good things about Charleston.

My day of discharge was June 1, 1967, and the beginning of our new work was July 1. During the months of May and June we traveled to Charleston to look for a home. Logically, the best place to look for church property was in a new development between Charleston and Summerville. Our search for a new home was halfway between the two cities, and it took us into many different neighborhoods. We were limited financially by how big a loan we could get from the G.I. Bill. Our dreams were more expensive than we could afford.

5813 Lakeview Drive Hanahan

While roaming the town of Hanahan, a small incorporated suburb just north of North Charleston, we saw a street named Lakeview Drive that seemed interesting even though we could not see a lake. There we saw a brick house with a well-manicured yard surrounded by many trees with a sign in the front that read "For sale by owner." We knew that the house would be far beyond our means, but we decided to stop and take a look just for fun. The home was owned by Mac and Lucille MacLennon. They were gracious enough to take us on a tour of the entire house. The backyard was manicured as well as the front yard. There was also a playhouse that had been built for their son and daughter, who were now teenagers. I could see Rose drooling as she walked from room to room. Well, we were just about to leave when I asked, more for curiosity, what the selling price was. Mac answered, "Somewhere around $40,000," which was far above our $30,000 limit. We thanked them for the tour of their home.

As we were walking out the door, Lucille, in her feisty manner, said, "Mac, Bob is a minister, my grandfather was a minister, and this house was blessed by a minister. I want Bob and Rose to have this house for whatever they can afford." Our search had ended. That is how we got our home in which we would spend most of the rest of our lives.

Mac and Lucille were moving to a new home in Charleston, but it would not be ready until September. Our plan was that Rose and the kids would stay in Darlington, I would rent an apartment in Charleston, and they would come on weekends.

I found a small apartment at 1 Meeting Street. My office was a park bench in White Point Garden, across the street, overlooking the Ashley and Cooper rivers as they drifted into the Atlantic Ocean. Here I was, a Presbyterian minister without a church or congregation and my family living a hundred miles away. I was excited to begin a new adventure in our life, but it was a lonely time in my ministry. I asked myself at times, sitting on the park bench, Wouldn't it have been better to seek a call from an established church or a residence as a hospital chaplain?

My first task was to begin the search for a suitable piece of land in an accessible part of the city to organize a church or find an existing church property that had become vacant. I began by calling some United Presbyterian ministers in Charleston. The majority of the churches were in suburbs or the country. Many of the ministers I called invited me to visit. They were cordial, but made it clear that a new United Presbyterian church in a white community was the idea of the national office and not of the Atlantic Presbytery. A few of the younger ministers were adamantly opposed to the plan. I was also informed that the presbytery would not officially oppose the plan because the national office supported the churches' presbytery by giving over $1 million a year. But I still thought it was a great program, so I pressed on.

Through the summer, I spent many hours with real estate folks looking for available property. I found a piece of land near Summerville in what was to be a planned community with all the amenities. There were several sites set aside just for churches. I had the Southeastern Conference minister look at the land and he agreed it looked like a good choice. I also took time to visit some of the churches that were in the Presbyterian Church (U.S.A), popularly known as the Southern Presbyterian Church. I was surprised to find what I would call ecclesiastical hostility. To quote one minister, "We are responsible for new churches' development in our area. We do not need the Northern Church to barge in on us." Even though I had spent the last eleven years as a minister and chaplain in the U.S. church I was not warmly received. At this point I really felt challenged. During these first three months, I met several families who were very much interested in a progressive church with an open-door policy.

I met and played tennis with Palmer Patterson, the minister of the Park Circle Presbyterian Church, which was in the Charleston Presbytery. When I told him my family could not come to Charleston because the home we purchased would not be ready until September, he invited us to stay in the church manse during August, as he and his family would be on vacation. We accepted the invitation. It was good to have the family with me again and my aloneness began to leave.

We moved into our home on September 1, 1968. It was an exciting time. Plans for the new development were escalating. I had made arrangements with a Catholic church on Dorchester Road to have services there until new facilities could be built. I had set December 1 as a target date. There were twelve families who had expressed a strong interest in organizing the church. All were Southern Presbyterians. I thought it was ironic that I was accepted more by the priest of a Roman Catholic church than by my fellow Presbyterians.

In early October I received a phone call from a Mr. Bill Sharpe, inviting me to have breakfast with him. We met at the Golden Eagle restaurant across the street from Circular Congregational Church on Meeting Street in downtown Charleston. Bill told me that he was a member of Circular and also the chairman of the pulpit nominating committee. Their minister, Dr. Bill Barnhart, had retired. My name was given to him by the United Church of Christ Southeastern Conference minister. He was told that I was a United Presbyterian minister in Charleston to organize a new church and I might be available to conduct worship services while the members of Circular Church decided what they were going to do. I gladly accepted the opportunity. I had not had the chance to preach a sermon or be with a congregation since leaving the army.

We agreed on two Sundays. Even though the congregation was small and most present were much older than I, I enjoyed the experience immensely. After the second Sunday, I was invited back for several more Sundays and asked to attend a few Standing Committee meetings to share my thoughts about church development and my personal views on Circular's situation.

At this time there were only thirty-seven active members. The church's two buildings were in dire need of repairs. Circular was surrounded within a few blocks by five large and active Protestant churches. The committee had for some time been deliberating on whether to redevelop in

Circular Family

their present location or sell their property and move to a suburban location. When asked for my thoughts, I told the Standing Committee members that if they were interested in remaining a traditional inner-city church they could not survive, but if there was a willingness and openness to develop programs that reached out to the community there was a good possibility of rebuilding. In my experience, established Protestant congregations in the South were more exclusive than inclusive, appealing more to their own kind.

At the Standing Committee's request I prepared a list of possible programs that would reach out to the community. I felt like a consultant in new church development, which was a comfortable position. I could make all kinds of suggestions for consideration without the responsibility to carry them out. Most of the committee members showed a keen interest in my long list of possible programs. As the meeting came to close, Bill Sharpe asked me what the possibility was that I would be interested in becoming their minister. My immediate reaction was to inform the committee that, first of all, I was a Presbyterian and I was under a contract to develop a new church in the Charleston area. Second, I knew very little about the policies and views of the United Church of Christ. Bill informed me that there were a number of churches in the country, including in North Carolina, Georgia, and Florida, that had formed union churches between both denominations. Ministers had a reciprocal arrangement to provide services for both denominations. I had not known of that development. It sounded good. After conducting services at Circular and visiting members in their homes, I was beginning to feel a bond with the church and especially with its history, openness to individuals of varied ethnic backgrounds, and a willingness to explore ways of serving the surrounding communities.

I shared the idea of a union between the two churches with my supervisor, the Southeastern executive minister of the United Presbyterian Church. He in turn discussed the idea with his counterpart in the UCC. Both thought it could be a good move for both churches. The resources already allotted for the Presbyterian development added to the existing resources of Circular Church would benefit the needs of both. The plan was submitted to the national office of the two denominations and was quickly approved. The small group of Presbyterians who were interested in the new development near Summerville joined Circular and developed a session of four elders to fulfill the requirement of the Southern Presbyterian Church. We had accomplished in a couple of months what had been envisioned to take five years.

CHAPTER TWENTY-TWO

CIRCULAR CONGREGATIONAL CHURCH

Circular 1970

The Circular congregation was small in numbers yet huge in congeniality, even though there were widespread differences in the members' educations and backgrounds. They were proud of their church's history. It had been founded in the 1680s by English Congregationalists, Scots Presbyterians, and French Huguenots, and was known as "The Dissenting Church." Early in the nineteenth century the church was the largest domed building in the country and housed about two thousand worshippers. That building was destroyed in a fire in 1861 and eventually the present church was built in 1890. The members planned, worked, and socialized together with very little dissension.

Here I sat in a semi-round office in the back of a round church, looking through stained-glass windows at the oldest graveyard in Charleston. Since I was no longer an interim minister and consultant, the responsibility was on me to decide where to begin. My first priority was to purchase office furniture for the pastor's study and a secretary's office. (The former minister did all his work in his home.) The second task was to find a church secretary to answer the phone, type letters, and print the bulletin for Sunday—and also to provide me with some company. Being alone in this cathedral was a little creepy at times.

The first task was easy; it only required a visit to a used-office-furniture store. The second task took a little more time. I had the good fortune of meeting a retired church secretary at a workshop at St. John's Lutheran Church, which was only a few blocks from Circular. Her name was Mary Chisolm, a lifelong Charlestonian and a Lutheran. When I told her my story of how I happened to become the new minister at Circular Church she readily acknowledged my need for help. She told me that she would not be able to work for long, as she had eye problems and at seventy-three years of age her energy was not what it used to be. She was not only an excellent secretary, she knew most of the ins and outs of Charleston life (a very complicated affair, as I would learn), and passed them on to me. She also had a mothering instinct for young ministers and their families. During most of the first few months as a young and new minister in an historical church I spent my time visiting former and inactive members and preparing for Sunday morning services.

After the Christmas holidays the Standing Committee began to consider ways the church could reach out to the community. The first venture to be considered was to develop an affiliation with Parents Without Partners, a national organization whose goal was to provide support and socialization for individuals who had been divorced or widowed. Four single parents, three women and one man, met in my office to explore the bylaws and requirements of the national organization. One of the four members was a woman whose husband had died the year before, leaving her with two teenagers. This chapter of PWP was started in Circular's Lance Hall. Letters and announcements were sent out to churches and schools. When we sent an announcement to be published in the Charleston *News and Courier* I discovered for the first time that Circular had been boycotted by the local paper because of its history of holding dissenting views, mostly around the issues of race relations, the equality of men and women, and the church's acceptance of different lifestyles. Despite the paper's refusal to publish an announcement, the chapter grew rapidly.

The next outreach program resulted from an action of the Charleston City Council. There was a coffee house on King Street named The Poet that catered mostly to teenagers who were popularly known then as hippies. Large numbers gathered day and night and stayed into the early hours of the morning. When merchants and residents on and around King Street began to complain about the noise these young people generated, the city fathers closed it down. During one of Circular's monthly sessions, a member brought up the question, "Where are all those young people going for fellowship and enjoyment?" In discussing the issue, a member brought up the idea of Lance Hall, which had been vacant for some time, as a possible place for the youth to have a coffeehouse. This idea brought further exploration.

After a meeting with several of the older young people who had been frequent patrons of The Poet, the result was the development of a coffeehouse named The Poet's Other, located in upper Lance Hall. The hours were from 10 o'clock until 10 o'clock, Monday through Saturdays. Rules were established, including no alcohol or drugs on the church property, and the coffeehouse would be thoroughly cleaned at closing time. Smoking would be allowed since the minister of the church smoked. The young people themselves were to be responsible for the daily operation

Young people at Circular

of the coffeehouse, including the purchase and preparation of food and drinks and the organization of the band.

The women of the church provided a potluck dinner for the opening day. To their surprise and embarrassment, more than two hundred young people showed up, when they had expected only twenty-five to fifty. After a last-minute rush to a local grocery store, every single serving plate was filled and cleaned. A question was raised at the next session meeting, "Has Circular taken on a project that is too big for a small congregation?"

Remembering back, it seems like it took the whole congregation to get the coffeehouse started and operating without any serious problems. Members volunteered to be present in the evenings and available if needed. The women of the church continued the Wednesday night potluck supper, with the support of other churches in the area.

A program was started following the supper featuring a professional who dealt with some of the issues young people were facing, such as the use and abuse of alcohol and drugs, mental-health issues, problem pregnancies, safety issues, spiritual issues, etc.

As I mingled on a daily basis with the young folks who were frequent customers, I discovered a wide diversity. Many were from dysfunctional families, and The Poets' Other was their way of finding a substitute family. Some were there just to have a place to be free, to be themselves, to dress as they chose, and to listen to the kind of music they enjoyed. Some were there to hide from a troubled past of juvenile delinquency. Some were from prominent and well-educated families, but felt excluded from their parents' social lives. I listened to occasional confessions, such as, "I don't like the life I have been living" and "I've done some bad things, Pastor." I heard about indiscriminate uses of sex and drugs. Overall, the program was considered successful by the congregation, city officials, and health professionals.

The coffeehouse adventure was the origin for other programs at Circular. There was the HOT LINE, which was recommended by the young people, a number they could call to ask for help with a variety of issues. The first phone was connected in the women's restroom underneath the coffeehouse. Volunteers from Circular, other churches, and professional services answered calls twenty-four hours a day. As calls increased, more phones were needed, and a larger office (outside of a restroom) was found. The United Way provided the funding.

A counseling program was started at the church for young people under sixteen who had run away from home. Ministers from other churches volunteered to serve as counselors. Many of these children had moved into small apartments where a number of young people lived together in what was called communes. These places were usually managed by adults who profited financially from homeless kids. I personally visited some of these communes because a number of the kids who came to the coffeehouse lived there. I found the living conditions deplorable. I reported them to the Charleston police chief who agreed to have the communes patrolled and inspected for child endangerment. Occasionally the more responsible young people who came to the coffeehouse brought young people to the runaway center with the encouragement to go back home or find a foster home.

A counseling program was started for unwed mothers to help them consider options to abortion. The church worked closely with the Florence Crittenton Home, where unwed mothers could live until their babies were born with the encouragement to give them up for adoption. The United Presbyterian Church had a center in Atlanta that provided counsel and an abortion as a last choice to avoid unhealthy solutions.

A counseling program was also organized to assist young boys seventeen and older to consider options to the draft into the armed forces. The war in Vietnam was escalating and a number of young men who considered themselves conscientious objectors left home and moved to Canada or other foreign countries to avoid the draft.

[On Bob's feelings about the war in Vietnam, Robin notes, "In reading Dad's letters I think you can see a definite change in his attitude towards the war. I don't know that he was ever for the war but felt compelled to serve due to his patriotic duty and calling to help people. He delivered several sermons about the war after his return. One was titled, 'Can Prayers Change the War?' He said several people left the church when he expressed his anti-war sentiments.]

Many stories came out of the coffeehouse, but there was one that had a lifetime effect on the culture of the congregation. At one of the Wednesday night suppers, Mrs. Agnes Kistler, the church historian and one of the oldest members of the church, said to me, "I want to say something to your young people." I worried about this a little, wondering what she wanted to say. Ms. Agnes was the epitome of prim and proper, always dressed exquisitely, and she carried a black cane with a gold top. Born in the nineteenth century, she was often referred to as "the Queen." When she stepped up on the band's platform the young folks began to chuckle. Ms. Agnes promptly tapped the top of her cane on the microphone until there was silence. She began by asking the question, "Has Reverend Boston ever invited you to come to church on Sunday?" The chuckling turned to laughter, as if she were joking. (I thought to myself, That wasn't a bad idea, even though I hadn't considered it myself.) Then she said, "I'm inviting you now. I think you might enjoy some of Reverend Boston's sermons." (More chuckling.) Then as she was leaving she came back to the microphone and tapped her cane until quiet returned and shared an afterthought, "If you should decide to come, make sure you dress like you are, not like we stuffy old folks do." More laughter.

On the very next Sunday twenty young folks came and sat in the back of the church, appearing as though they were having a sit-in. When the service ended, many in the congregation went over and invited these strange visitors to join them for refreshments in the back of the sanctuary. Then on the following Sunday a few came back and to my amazement several of the men of the church came without wearing ties and a few women had on slacks, something unheard of in that day and time. A new dress code had been established at Circular Church. Come as you are!

Through all of this, membership and attendance at Circular Church was increasing, which I believe was a result of the acceptance of The Poet's Other coffeehouse and our other community activities.

And our family's size was increasing, too, as Rose gave birth to our third child, Richard, on December 18, 1970, in Charleston. Unfortunately for ministers like me, no insurance covered births so we had to remit a down payment to the hospital early. It was a busy time in all the hospitals, so Rose's doctor sent her to another hospital. Because of Rusty's quick birth, the doctor met her there, but this birth went by the book. The doctor sat by Rose's bed and timed every movement with his new Swiss Rolex watch. [Rose remembers: "I saw each of my first two children when they were four hours old, because of the gas that kept me under. I administered my own "gas" this time by clicking a button, so I was awake when Richard was born. I saw him before Bobby and announced, 'We have another T-Ball player!' Robin and Rusty took him over for most of his early years. He even has the distinction of being the first child born to a minister while at Circular Church. How is that for being historic?]

When the church secretary Mary Chisolm announced that it was time for her to retire again, she recommended a Lutheran friend, Jean Lofton, as a replacement. Jean had secretarial experience and was an active church member. Jean not only served as secretary of the church but also as administrator of the counseling services that the church was offering to the community.

Life for me was beginning to settle down and I enjoyed just being a pastor of an historical church that was beginning a new history. My enjoyment at just being a pastor did not last long. Another program that developed out of the coffeehouse was a radio talk show involving Dr. George Orvin, an adolescent psychiatrist from the Medical University of South Carolina and myself. WJMX, a local radio station that catered to teenagers and young adults, invited

Dr. Orvin and me to have a one-hour program concerning teenagers. It was called, "A conversation between a psychiatrist and a minister on the problems young people are facing today." During the last thirty minutes young people and parents were invited to call in to make a comment or ask a question. We were also invited by WCSC television, an affiliate of CBS, to have the same program. This program generated a number of unexpected calls from parents and teenagers to Circular Church.

The result was the development of the first Marriage and Family Center in Charleston. The offices were set up in Lance Hall, with a nursery and an adult class on Sunday. Jean Lofton, the secretary, served both the church and the counseling center. Since I had previous training in family therapy, I became the temporary director. The center grew to the point where a full-time director was going to be needed. A search committee led by Dr. Kathryn Sharpe, who was the chair of the Sociology Department at Baptist College (later Charleston Southern University) and a longtime member of Circular Church, was organized. (Kaye's husband, Bill Sharpe, was the head of the Standing Committee who first invited me to Circular.) In the process of interviewing pastoral counselors from both U.C.C. and Presbyterian churches I decided to accept the full-time director's position. I was coming to the end of my five-year commitment to the Board of National Missions of the United Presbyterian Church and I enjoyed my work with the counseling center. In addition, being a full-time counselor was closer to what I had envisioned when I finished seminary. Not having to write a sermon every Sunday was also an incentive.

The transition from being the minister of the church to the director of the counseling center was made possible by the help of Rev. Albert Keller, the Presbyterian chaplain for the colleges and universities in the Charleston area. Bert had attended Circular on a number of occasions and assisted in the work of the Runaway Center. He had conducted services on several occasions and was well liked by the congregation. With the church's agreement, in 1974 Bert and I agreed to alternate conducting services in order for the counseling center to become financially independent. At the end of the year Bert assumed the responsibility of being a part-time pastor of the church while limiting his campus work to the Medical University of South Carolina.

As the young people who started the coffeehouse grew older it began to lose its appeal for some of those who had attended it, but I never forget what it had done for the congregation and me personally.

During the year of 1974, Kaye Sharpe and I traveled to Columbia on a weekly basis to pursue accreditation with the American Association of Marriage and Family Therapy. Our supervisor was Rev. Paul Carlson, director of the counseling center at the Trenholm Road Methodist Church in Columbia. In addition, I decided to pursue a master's degree in family education at Southern Illinois University, which had a program located on the Charleston Air Force Base. This was a two-year accelerated program conducted on weekends. In 1974 the Marriage and Family Counseling Center became financially self-supporting. At that time, I resigned as minister of the church and became full-time director of the center. Bert became the minister of the church on a part-time basis while continuing his work with the Medical University.

An article in the *Charleston Magazine* in December 1975 explained some of my activities: "The man behind the service is busy, but untiring. His appointment schedule stays full, and in addition to his primary duties he is active in professional counseling seminars; he consults with other counseling organizations, teaches in the Departments of Family Practice and Behavioral Science at the Medical University and does special counseling with groups of college and high school students."

During the next three years it became necessary to add another counselor to the staff. Unfortunately, Circular did not have the space for an additional office. Dr. Phillip Noble, minister of the First (Scots) Presbyterian Church, and an ardent supporter of the Counseling Center, invited us to look at a vacant old carriage house on the church property as a possible location for the center. Since First (Scots) was only a few blocks away, this would have been a good opportunity for the growth of the center. We were very disappointed when the session of the church rejected the plan. I had wanted the center to have a close association with a church.

Finding it more and more difficult to work alone in a family counseling situation, I accepted an invitation to join a group practice in the West Ashley area with Dr. Diana Rosen, a psychiatrist, and William Quesenbery, a child psychologist. I continued to maintain a close association with ministers and churches. I started a program with individual congregations similar to the employee assistance program of many companies. The churches contributed to the program and I saw the members at a reduced fee. In addition, I had an ongoing support group for Presbyterian and Lutheran ministers.

CHAPTER TWENTY-THREE

A DARK PERIOD IN MY JOURNEY

This transition away from the church and to the counseling center in part was a celebration professionally and at the same time a soul-searching and heartbreaking experience personally. I felt at times a bit schizoid, two people living in one body, a pastoral counselor during the day and a husband and father at night and on holidays. The parenting side was always good; Rose and I were with the kids at every special activity at school and on the ballfields. They were with us on all of our vacations. We were the picture of an All-American family. Yet as a married couple we failed each other. Here I was, a successful minister and a marriage-and-family supervisor, but personally I was experiencing what felt like a broken marriage. Rose was enjoying success as an academic counselor at Baptist College. She had her social life with her friends and colleagues and I had my own friends. We had a few married friends who we enjoyed together. But when we were alone together, there was a mixture of silence, criticism, hurt, and anger. We blamed each other for our lack of intimacy and enjoyment as a couple.

I had suggested several times that we needed to go to a marriage counselor, but her response was, "All the therapists know you." Our conflict went on for several years. I felt we needed to do something different. The expressions of hurt and anger were escalating. We were at a stalemate.

In the literature for marriage-and-family counseling there is an option suggested for a dysfunctional marriage. Instead of deciding on divorce or staying in a marriage for the sake of the children or for financial reasons, a trial separation can be therapeutic. A couple agrees on certain times for the separation to begin and end. Three months was considered as an ideal time, long enough to consider what living apart would be like and short enough not to disrupt positive aspects of family life. Open communication between husband and wife is recommended and the relationships with the children should remain as normal as possible. The couple must agree that there will not be any sexual encounter with another person.

When I presented the idea to Rose, her response was, "If that's what you want, do it." At the time, we owned a Winnebago motorhome. I packed enough clothes to last me a couple of weeks. Rose helped me. She even gave me some food staples from our pantry. I left on a Sunday and the only tears I remember were those of Richard, who was around eight years old at the time. Robin, who was nineteen, and Rusty, being seventeen, probably thought it was a good idea. They must have been tired of hearing their mother and dad arguing so much of the time.

As I remember, it was on a cold day in the last part of February 1978 or '79. I wanted to get through Christmas before leaving. Then after Christmas I decided to wait until after Rusty's birthday, February 20. I remember it was Sunday evening when I started our motorhome, which was located on the right-of-way of the powerlines directly behind our home. I recall thinking that the Winnebago was seldom used without the family, so now I was all alone. It was a sad moment. I had said my goodbyes at the house, hugged everyone, including Rose, and told them I would see them at Rusty's basketball game on Tuesday. We had never missed a special activity of our kids and I was not going to miss one now.

I had not planned where I was going to park that night away from home. So I drove into Charleston and parked in the parking lot next to the church, which was dark and empty. It was time to settle in for the night. Since I was still working at the counseling center, I thought this would be a good place, since I had a full schedule for Monday and I was only a few yards from the office. I had brought several books to read, but as the dark settled in I began to feel uneasy in this part of the city. There were no cell phones to call 911. With no other place to go, I drove back to the right-of-way behind our house, hoping no one in the family would hear or see me. I didn't want them to think I had chickened out. I had a hard time going to sleep, not out of fear but thinking about what the next three months would bring. I thought about a little book I had read entitled *Jonathan Livingston Seagull*, by Richard Bach. It was a story about a seagull that decides he is tired of being just a beach scavenger, so he leaves his brother and sisters and soars the skies alone to find his freedom. I identified with him.

The next morning, with only a few hours of sleep, I went to work, hoping no one had noticed my presence. This trial separation was not getting off to a good start. But the next night was better. I found a motorhome park off of Highway 17 and had a good night's sleep. I usually sleep well after not sleeping the night before. One of my first dilemmas came about when I was starting another "Learning to Love Again" group. This was usually six to eight men and women who found themselves single again either by death of the partner, divorce, or separation. The question I asked myself: Do I tell them I am separated? I remember during the introductions I told them and gave them the option to drop out. No one did and I also got a lot of support.

Over the next few weeks I settled into a comfortable routine. Several colleagues invited me to stay in their homes. I accepted a couple because it would help to avoid the night doldrums of loneliness and a diet of fast food. I stayed only a couple of days in order not to interfere with their family routines. I still had the mixed emotions of enjoying a sense of freedom and an absence of marital discord, along with a sense of failure that we couldn't find a suitable solution to our own marriage. I accepted one invitation and stayed for a few weeks, in a cottage on Seabrook Island that was vacant for the winter. The place had an atmosphere similar to what I imagine the Garden of Eden was like. I invited the kids one by one to spend the night but only Richard accepted. The others were busy with their own lives.

I continued to follow the guidelines of a trial separation by calling Rose at least once a week and keeping up with the kids. I could not help but notice a change in Rose's attitude. I didn't notice any anger or expression of hurt. She asked about my health and how I was doing. I asked her about having lunch with me and she accepted. We talked amiably about the kids and our mutual friends. I got to thinking, Maybe this separation is working. I must admit I thought about someday having a partner who shared some of my individual interests, like sailing, hiking, playing tennis or golf, and exercising. Yet at the same time was the realization of how much Rose's and my different strengths made up for our individual shortcomings.

The three months seemed to pass quickly. I enjoyed my freedom from our marital conflicts, but missed just being together with the family. I knew that if I decided to continue the separation and work toward a divorce, it would take a year before it would become legal, since neither of us had grounds for a divorce.

During the last few weeks of our trial separation, Fred Wichmann, a former client, invited me to help crew his sailboat to the Bahamas. He was an experienced sailboat captain and I had made many trips to the Bahamas on his fifty-two-foot schooner. He said I could invite a friend to go along. I was ready for a vacation. I accepted the invitation and invited my best friend, Jake Hughes, to go on the trip, which was scheduled to last about three weeks. At the time, I was leaning towards extending the separation. I vowed to myself I would make a decision before I returned to Charleston.

We left Folly Beach at twilight on a warm, sunny day in June and headed toward the Gulf Stream, which according to our captain would give us the current we needed to reach the Bahama Islands in four days. I had recently learned a little about sailing at a school run by the Charleston Coast Guard and had taken several trips in our twenty-five-foot O'Day sailboat named *Windsong* that our family had bought in partnership with Dr. Bill Quesenbery, a colleague in the family-counseling field. Fred's *Mobjack* was more than twice as long as *Windsong,* with sails three times as big. I was an inexperienced deck hand, following orders from the captain. If my memory is right, it took us about four to five hours to reach the Gulf Stream by motor. I was excited and for a few hours I completely forgot about family, work, and life back in Charleston. As the lights on land became dimmer and the sun disappeared, the day was turning into a clear night, with stars and the moon bright. The only distraction was the motor on the boat. I recall it was sometime around midnight when the captain turned off the motor and raised the sails. I began to experience the silence of the night along with the wind, which was turning us southward into a world I had never known.

There were four of us on board, including the captain, his brother-in-law, and my friend Jake. We each took a three-hour watch at the helm. A major concern at night was cruise or merchant ships in the area. That first night was beautiful. The stars remained in their places. The moon wandered from here to there and the ship sailed windward. Jake and I took our watches together, which meant staying awake and alert for six hours. With our excitement, we would not have been able to sleep anyway.

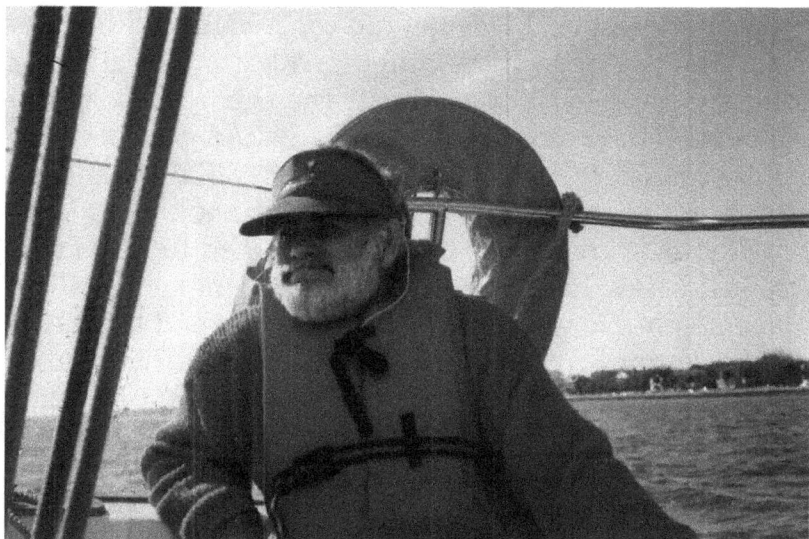

Sailing WindSong

I think it was sometime around 3 o'clock in the morning I told Jake that I was thinking about extending my separation with Rose. He didn't respond and continued looking into the distance. Jake and Geri had been Rose and my close friends for many years. Every week we did something together, having breakfast or dinner, going to garage sales or on camping trips. Jake and Geri were part of our family and we were part of theirs. After a few moments of no response I asked Jake, "Did you hear what I said?" He finally responded, "I prefer not to talk about it," as we sailed on to the sound of the sea and the wind. The next day went as planned. Jake appeared to ignore my presence.

The following night began as the night before, the wind still at our backs, the sea smooth, the weather perfect. Then shortly after midnight, with Jake and me on watch, the captain emerged from his berth in the bow of the boat and announced, "Turn on the motors, we have a leak in the front, and we need to turn west toward land." Our orders were: one person at the helm, all others bailing the water in the galley. I was not too concerned, as I had no-ticed a fairly large rubber dinghy with a motor attached sitting in the middle of the boat. Then came the disturb-ing news. The motor on the dinghy would not start. The bailing couldn't keep up with the water coming in and the calculation to reach land was six to eight hours. Sudden-ly, without warning, our excitement turned to fear. Panic was just below the surface. I could hear the not-so-silent prayers, that the weather would stay clear and the motor would continue running. The captain also reported that he could not get a clear reception on the ship-to-shore radio.

The next few hours were terrifying. We took turns in the stern behind the big wheel while the other three continued to bail. We squinted to the west, longing to see the first lights of land. Jake and I wondered why an experienced seaman would begin such a journey without checking the emergency equipment. (We would later learn that almost all of the sailors at the James Island Yacht Club had had similar experiences with Fred. That was why his nickname was "Captain Crunch.") As the *Mobjack* rambled toward the invisible shore, I thought about Rose, Robin, Rusty, Richard, and Penny, our lovable dachshund. I longed for a hug from each one. We waited, we wandered, we prayed.

Then it happened. Joy replaced our fear when someone shouted, "I see a light!" At that moment, we didn't care if it was a ship or a shore. Soon we discovered it was the land, St. Augustine, Florida. Pulling into the marina, we were exuberant, except for our captain who was thinking of the hole in his boat and the journey ahead.

After a few inquiries, Fred said it would take a day or more to have the *Mobjack* repaired. Jake and I took our duffel bags and headed into the city to find a place to eat break-fast. Even after two nights without sleep we were still wide awake and thankful we were on land. The first night in St. Augustine we found a reasonable hotel and had our first night of sleep in two days. The following day we continued our tour, visiting historic churches in the area. At the end of the second day we went back to the boat. The captain informed us we would be sailing the next morning. I had already decided I didn't want to get aboard that boat again. My excuse was that with a three-day delay I would not get back in time to meet my appointments. The captain told Jake, "You're not going to leave us, too?" Jake replied, "I'm with him"; it was obvious he did not want to continue our journey either.

We had planned to stay in the motel that last night, but I told Jake I wanted to leave for home as soon as we could, if we could find a way. I remember Jake asking, "Where is home?" I told him I wanted to go back and live with Rose and the kids. I saw a smile on Jake's face followed by a big hug.

We checked the train station, but no train was scheduled that evening. But at the bus station, we were told that one was leaving at 11 o'clock that evening and was to arrive in Charleston at 8 in the morning. Before buying our tickets, I called Rose and told her that I wanted to come home if it would be okay with her. I think her answer was something like, "We're still here." I asked her if she would meet us at the bus station in the morning at 8 o'clock. She said, "We'll be there."

We arrived at the Charleston bus station at 8 o'clock. As the bus pulled into the station, I saw Rose, Robin, Rusty, and Richard standing on the outside. Before I got my duffel bag under the bus, I got those four hugs I had been craving.

Geri was at the station to meet Jake. As we drove home, no one mentioned anything about our separation. We stopped at McDonald's for breakfast before driving home. After getting home everyone returned to their normal routines. Rose made sandwiches for lunch. I struggled to decide how to break the silence of our separation and tell Rose I wanted to end our separation and together find the peace and joy and love we once had. I think she knew from the phone conversation from St. Augustine, but she didn't mention it. I r member trying not to sound like a counselor when I asked her if she would be more comfortable if I slept on the couch my first night at home, emphasizing "*my first*." I remember her answer, "Our bed is still big enough for both of us."

Our first week back together was peaceful. Rose went to her work at the college and I stayed at home since I still had a couple of weeks left on my vacation. We didn't talk about the past three months, yet there was no criticism, anger, or hurt expressed by either of us. Most of our post-separation conversations centered on the kids and home activities. We did come to an agreement that we would schedule one night a week for just the two of us to do something fun and that we would find a counselor who did not know either of us. I was glad to be home again and Rose appeared to be accepting as well.

During the rest of the summer we took several trips to the mountains, both with the kids and just Rose and me. The trip I enjoyed the most was when we took three days without reservations as to where we would stop or sleep. My brother Ronnie loaned us his MGB convert-

Pisgah Inn

Pisgah Inn, NC on our anniversary

ible. That's how we discovered the Pisgah Inn on the Blue Ridge Parkway. I enjoyed telling people we met along the way, despite Rose's embarrassment, that "we just got married and we're on our honeymoon." That first night at the Pisgah Inn was the beginning of an annual trip that we took for the next thirty years.

There were other events that had a renewed effect on our marriage. We attended a marriage-enrichment retreat in Winston-Salem, North Carolina, and enjoyed it so much that Rose and I went to a training session to lead marriage-and-family retreats ourselves. We were invited to lead a number of retreats over the next several years.

The addition to my practice of leading marriage-enrichment retreats was a welcomed experience. It gave Rose and me the opportunity to spend some delightful weekends in romantic places away from the kids. Our marital problems were not over yet, but we were finding healthy ways to move through them.

In 1985 I was elected president of the South Carolina Association of Marriage and Family Therapy. This was a great opportunity to travel throughout the state visiting other centers and therapists. It also gave us an opportunity to go to annual national conferences. Rose and I had memorable experiences in New York, San Francisco, and Montreal. This also gave me the chance to work with the legislature of South Carolina to enact a bill giving professional counselors and marriage-and-family counselors the right to receive third-party payments from insurance companies. It took two years, but it passed. That was my one and only involvement with politics.

Hugo

In September 1989 Hurricane Hugo hit Charleston, flooding streets, uprooting trees, and tearing roofs from houses. Robin and Rosalyn came home, because our house was more substantial than theirs. We spent a terrifying night together. [Robin remembers: "For anyone who went through it, Hugo changed our perspectives for a long time. Rosalyn was two and we were living about three blocks away from Mom and Dad. Richard was at Clemson, and Rusty lived in Greenville. Mom and Dad begged us to come to their house, so we did. When the worst of the storm came, we were cut off from the phone while talking to Rusty and had no power, only a battery-operated radio that went in and out while the wind howled outside. We all bunked on mattresses in the hallway and closet. I didn't know whether to get on top of Rosalyn (where I might have crushed her) or hold her tight. I remember my father was reciting the Lord's Prayer when we heard what sounded like a bomb hit the house. The biggest oak tree in Hanahan knocked off the corner of the house. It looked like something from a movie, when something smashes a hole in an airplane. Dad told me this was the scariest moment of his life, even more than when bombs were exploding in Vietnam because then he didn't have to worry about us. This even taught us what is important in life, that we are not in control, and that all our worldly possessions can be blown away at any moment.]

Richard was then a freshman at Clemson University, and he came home two days after Hugo in his small Toyota truck with food, water, and other needed supplies, along with cash that he had reserved for his food. My heart burst with love and joy.

While at home in the days following the hurricane, I realized my phones at home and at the office had stopped ringing. No phones, no patients. No patients, no money, though the bills continued to come. I felt like I had been fired without severance pay. My office was closed for three weeks. I went into the tree business without pay, as we lost numerous trees in our yard.

CHAPTER TWENTY-FOUR

CHARLESTON FAMILY SERVICES AND LUTHERAN FAMILY COUNSELING CENTER

It was not long after Hugo that I was offered a position with Charleston Family Services, a United Way agency. Most of my work with Family Services was as the director of the Employee Assistance Program. I enjoyed working with some of the major companies in Charleston and their employees. One of the most difficult assignments was to provide counseling for the employees of a bank that had experienced the emotional trauma of a robbery. The best part of working with Family Services was that the staff worked together as a family and we learned from each other. The front office took care of the bookkeeping and finances.

I was with Charleston Family Services for about four years when I was asked by Lutheran Family Services of North Carolina to develop a Lutheran Family Counseling Center somewhere in the greater Charleston area. I had become familiar with the Lutheran Church years earlier. For ten years I had a support group with six Lutheran pastors. This group had its beginning when several pastors asked if I would meet with them in my office to discuss ways of dealing with troubled parishioners. Originally the group was to meet for an hour and a half once a week for six weeks. After the first six weeks, some of the individuals expressed the desire to continue meeting. In reality, the group changed to a support group for the six pastors. It also became a support group for me and for this reason I no longer charged a fee. We developed a close friendship with each other. Once a year we invited our spouses to join us for a dinner at a special restaurant. The group gave me a T-shirt that read "Honorary Lutheran."

It felt good to be able to work with a church again. As director I was given a full salary with an office large enough to add other counselors and a full-time secretary. Over the next two years, three counselors were added to the staff and a satellite center was opened in Mount Pleasant. The counseling center became financially self-supporting. Every Lutheran church in the city became a part of the membership-assistance program. The Charleston Atlantic Presbytery wrote into its budget funds for a ministers' support group. The majority of my time was spent seeing counselors in groups and individual sessions to become licensed as Presbyterian marriage-and-family counselors. The center had a contract with the Department of Mental Health to supervise their new mental-health counselors. It became necessary to find new offices to accommodate a growing staff.

Rose and I continued to lead marriage-enrichment retreats throughout South Carolina and North Carolina. We were even invited by a Lutheran Church in Miami. I especially enjoyed being a presenter at the South Carolina School of Alcohol and Drug Studies for several years, which was held at Furman University.

It was during this first year at the Lutheran Center, on January 23, 1993, that our family experienced the death of my mother, who was called Granny by everyone in the family. She died from a blood clot in her left leg. Her physician reported that they could give her a few more years if they took off her leg. She said no and the family agreed with her. She was seventy-nine years old and had been the stabilizing factor, physically, mentally, and spiritually, for the families of her three children. She visited each family once every three months, but stayed only three days. She alternated Christmases and her three families gathered at her house every Thanksgiving. She left me a legacy I'll always remember. I have always remembered her reminding me, "Remember, wherever you are, God is always with you." My sister Joy now carries her mantle and keeps the family together by organizing a family reunion every spring.

I was with Lutheran Counseling for six years; working with a team of counselors and sharing difficult cases was for me a learning and fun experience. I had planned to retire when I was sixty-seven but it was hard to leave such a great group of counselors. But when I reached sixty-nine I was ready to see if I could play golf again. The Lutheran Family Services of North Carolina put on a retirement party for me at Circular Church and gave me a rocking chair.

CHAPTER TWENTY-FIVE

SO-CALLED RETIREMENT

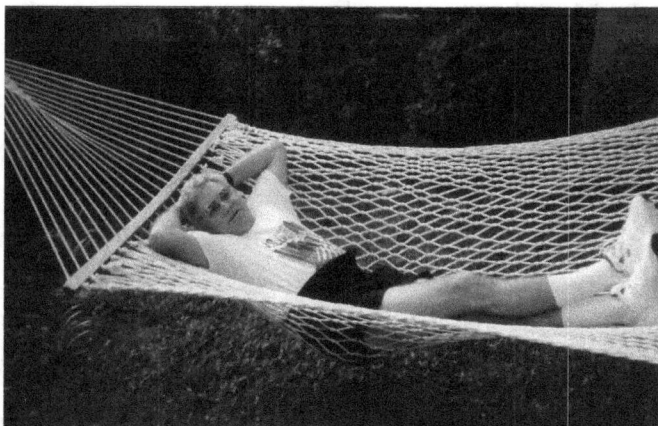

Relaxing on Lakeview

I was excited about retirement, having heard many times the old saying, "I am busier now than when I was working for a living." I was determined not to let this happen to me. I joined a group of seniors who played golf at the Charleston Municipal Golf Course three days a week. A few months after my retirement, Wayne Young, a Lutheran minister who had been in our support group, asked if I would be willing to take his place as a part-time chaplain for Lutheran Hospice, as he had been called as pastor to serve a Lutheran church. Having heard many good things about Hospice, I told him I would do so until they found a new chaplain. Two years later I retired again, almost too old to play golf three times a week.

My experience working with Hospice, meeting and being with individuals and families experiencing the intimacy of death, was both an honor and an enriching experience. My first hospice visit took me back emotionally years before when I had been asked to visit Ruth Adam, a member of my first church in Kansas City, who was dying of cancer and knew it. My experience as a hospice chaplain brought back that lesson, listening and responding rather than trying to decide what to say when visiting someone ill.

Ministry at the Village

When the time came to retire again, I got a phone call from an old friend who lived at the Presbyterian Village in Summerville. She asked if I would consider an interim chaplain position while the home searched for a new chaplain. This was a full-time position, with services on Sundays and Wednesday evenings, conducting funerals, which averaged two to three a week, in addition to daily visitations in the health care clinic. Inez Mitchum, the chair of the Chaplain Research Committee, thought a new chaplain would be found within a month or two. In considering the invitation, I thought the Village was the place where Rose and I would move sometime in the future and this would be a good opportunity to get to know what living there would be like. In addition, the added income would be helpful, and one to two months would come and go quickly. Five years later, following a serious heart attack after conducting six funerals in one week, I knew it was time to retire again. For real this time. Two days in the VA Hospital and my blood pressure returned to normal.

Reflecting back, these five years were the most spiritually enlightening time of my ministry. The residents of the Village taught me how to grow older gracefully and have joy, peace, and serenity along the way. And through much of my time there I had a good friend by my side. My time at the Village might best be summarized by a story I wrote for *Vantage*, the quarterly alumni magazine of Columbia Theological Seminary, and which was also published by the *Summerville Journal Scene*.

"HOLLY'S MINISTRY"

On Christmas Day in 1999 a five-week-old golden retriever came into our home. She was a retirement present from my wife. Providentially, a new career was about to begin.

When Holly was three years old and just out of her puppy and adolescent stage, I was asked to supply at the Presbyterian Village, a retirement community in Summerville, South Carolina. While they were seeking a new chaplain, I agreed to come for a couple of months if I could bring my dog. We stayed for five years.

From our very first day, Holly was received with open arms. Her gentleness, charm, and unconditional love, along with her wistful eyes and golden retriever perpetual smile, won the hearts of both staff and residents. Holly accompanied me on my visits throughout the Village. She seemed to possess an intuitive sense as to who liked dogs and who did not. She approached those who did (approximately 90 percent) by putting her head at their side, in their lap, or on the side of the bed, depending on the circum-

Me and Holly 1984

stance. She walked quietly by those who did not seem to care for dogs.

Some of Holly's best work could be seen in the Alzheimer's unit. There were incidents when residents were having difficult or uncontrollable times. Holly, sensing their discomfort, went to them, allowing the residents to begin talking to her while stroking her head, bringing a moment of calm. Often a resident talked to Holly when he or she was unable to communicate with staff or family, prompting nurses to call for Holly in stressful times.

When Holly was not with me, she could be found in the chaplain's office, lying on her pallet with a bowl of wa-

Me and Holly on the Mountain

ter by her side. Residents often dropped by to give her a pet, hug, or treat. Those times when I was without Holly, I was greeted more times than not with, "Where's Holly?" When Holly was with me, she was always greeted first. I mentioned this to a group of residents, prompting a dear sweet lady to say, "Maybe it's because Holly knows how to say I love you by wagging her tail instead of her mouth." There is a lot of wisdom in that pun. The late Bob Tapp, the founder and first president of the Summerville Presbyterian Home (now called The Village at Summerville), was fond of calling Holly the chaplain, while I was her assistant.

Donna Glisson, an independent resident, made Holly a scarf with an embroidered cross to match the stoles worn by the choir. She wore the scarf whenever she attended worship services. On numerous occasions Holly was invited by a family to attend a memorial service. This she did with grace and dignity. There was one exception. While sitting at attention at the graveside in the National Cemetery in Beaufort, South Carolina, when the first shot of a twenty-one-gun salute was fired, Holly began to bark. And there were twenty more shots to follow!

Holly the minister

I retired again in June 2007 for health reasons. There was an unspoken sentiment heard, "We can find a new chaplain, but we can't replace Holly." I retired, but Holly has continued to work. While we were still at the Village, Holly was evaluated by an observer from Ther-

Holly the Reading dog

apy Dogs Inc. She passed with honors and became a nationally registered therapy dog, which allows her access and privileges in many public places and institutions.

In addition, Holly is nationally registered as a Reading Education Assistance Dog (READ). Research has shown that children who read to animals learn more quickly and comprehend better because animals listen attentively, don't judge, laugh, or criticize, and allow children to proceed at their own pace. Holly has been going to the Hanahan Elementary School on Wednesday mornings for the past two years, listening to first-grade students read. Following her reading class, Holly visits a self-contained class of autistic children. This is her favorite class, as the students are rewarded dog treats for good behavior so they can treat Holly on Wednesdays. An eight-year-old boy spoke in class for the first time when he saw Holly. He said loudly, "Doggie," and has continued to add to his vocabulary.

Holly was also registered in the therapy program at the Children's Hospital of the Medical University of South Carolina and the Veterans Administration Hospital in Charleston. Along with her work with children, Holly makes grand rounds every Friday morning at the VA nursing home and mental-health clinic, and visits individual rooms.

A CBS television station in Charleston periodically rewards individuals for distinguished service to the community by nominating them as members of the Channel 5 Hall of Fame. Holly was the first dog ever to receive the award.

When her official duties are done, her work continues, as she comes home in the evenings to join her mom and dad for "happy hour," curling up in her favorite leather chair, while staying alert for anyone who might approach our home. All the while she provides stress relief, lowers blood pressure, and improves health in general, with her unconditional love for two old people enjoying their retiring years. At the age of seventy-five, I retired for the third time. I continued to take Holly on visits to hospitals, nursing homes, and schools.

Holly was also responsible for the development of a beautiful relationship in my life some years ago. As a volunteer and a patient at the VA Hospital in Charleston, I was walking down the hall to visit veterans in their rooms when a nurse started walking toward me. When she got in front of us, she asked, "Can I pet your dog?" I told her, "Sure, that's her job. She's a therapy dog to bring smiles and joy to patients and staff." At that moment she got down on her knees and hugged Holly. When she got up, I noticed she had tears in her eyes. She apologized and told me she had taken her golden retriever to the vet to be put to sleep just this past week. Then she asked, "When you and Holly visit the hospital, would you bring her by my office, so I can pet her and give her a hug?" I assured her that I would. So, for the next four to six years, usually on Friday, we stopped by Carol's station for Holly to get her hug. And sometimes I got a hug, too.

The time came when Holly became too old to walk the halls at the VA hospital and soon after we had to put her to sleep. She was thirteen years old, which in human terms was ninety-one. It was not long after Holly died that I was diagnosed with chronic leukemia and was instructed to report to a nurse in the Oncology-Hematology Department and she would set up and manage a treatment program for me. Emotionally distraught and scared, I reported. Astonishingly, Mrs. Carol Larson was the same nurse who had been hugging Holly—and sometimes me—for the past several years and she gave me a hug and assured me that I would get the best of care. Over the next several months Carol made herself available to me, Rose, and the family to answer questions and give us the encouragement we needed. She treated me the way she would treat her own father, who died when Carol was young. In appreciation, we invited Carol to go to church and out to dinner one Sunday. She shared with us her family story. Since that day, Carol has been a part of our family and has joined us on holidays and special times.

Me and Carol, Tilly, Shiloh and Wendy

CHAPTER TWENTY-SIX

A MIRACLE GIFT—ROBIN'S STORY

The accident—11-16-2016

This story began on a cool fall morning a week before Thanksgiving in 2016. Rose and I had just finished breakfast when we received a strange phone call from an unknown source. The first words were, "Who am I speaking with?" in a hurried, broken-English sort of manner. I responded, "With whom do you want to speak?" I thought the caller sounded like a salesman of some kind and I should hang up. But I let him talk. His next words were, "Are you a father?" I knew then that this was a crank call, yet I was still curious. He continued, "There is a lady who was driving a white car who has been in a serious accident. She gave me this number." Overwhelmed with shock and disbelief I asked where the accident happened. He told me, "Just over the Don Holt Bridge on Clements Ferry Road, about a mile towards Highway 41." He also described the intersection and said, "You better hurry."

Panic began to take hold. Scared and lost for words, we got in the car and drove as fast as we could to Clements Ferry Road in Mount Pleasant. As we approached, all we could see were trucks and cars at a standstill. Red and blue lights were flashing in the distance. We somehow managed to drive on the other side of the road, hoping the police would stop us and take us all the way. Surprisingly, we drove right up to Robin's car. It was a ball of mangled crushed steel. Directly behind it was a blue eighteen-wheeler. I had this numbing thought that no one could be living who was riding in that car and hoping that it was not Robin's car. While I stared in disbelief at the car, Rose was looking at the ambulance from MUSC, which was about twenty-five yards away. A police officer escorted her toward the ambulance.

When I got to the ambulance, there was Robin in the back, strapped to a gurney, her face covered with broken glass, her eyes open with a look of "Where am I and what are you doing here?" She was alive!

Rose rode in the ambulance with the driver. I followed. When I arrived at the hospital, Robin had already been taken into the trauma unit. Rose was in the waiting room. I called Robin's husband Bobby, and we waited nervously and frightened for the next three hours. Every time a person wearing a coat and tie walked into the waiting room we wondered with fear, Could that be a chaplain coming to console us with dreaded news? Finally, a nurse approached us with the message, "One of you can go in and see your daughter."

Then came the final and unexpected diagnosis. After every part of her body was x-rayed and examined, she only had a minor concussion and a cut lip. She was ready to go home.

We left the hospital in a state of excitement and disbelief, except Robin, who was still dressed in her paper hospital suit. She wanted to find her car and retrieve her personal belongings. After calling the Charleston police, we located her car at Jennings Towing Service. When we reached the salvage yard, the secretary met us with the condolence, "I am so sorry for the loss of your daughter," to which Robin replied, "No, I'm right here." The secretary said she had seen the car and couldn't believe that anyone who was in it could have survived. We were escorted to the back of the salvage yard where the car was parked and discovered that it was so crushed and mangled that nothing could be retrieved. We took Robin home.

I located the strange phone number from that morning and called the man who had told us of the wreck to thank him. When he answered, his first words were, "Is she alive?" When I told him yes, he said, "Thanks to God. Hallelujah! Hallelujah. I prayed for her when I saw her go under the truck and I have been praying for her ever since that moment." When he asked how she was doing, assuming she was still at the hospital, I told him, "She's already home. Would you like to talk to her?"

This phone call was the beginning of a new lifetime friendship. The caller's name was Raymond Young. Professionally, he is a truck driver and a minister at the Rock Hill Baptist Church in Moncks Corner. After talking to Robin, he shared with me what he had experienced. As I recall the conversation, he said:

"I saw the entire accident from beginning to the end. I was right behind the dump truck that pushed her car under a flatbed eighteen-wheeler filled with steel while she was stopped at a red light. When I got out of my truck, the police had taped off a space around the car to prevent people from peering at the woman trapped inside, who they assumed was dead due to the condition of the car. I stood outside the tape, about fifty feet from the car. The police and a wrecking crew were towing the dump truck and flatbed away, leaving Robin's car in the middle of the highway. Most of the crowd had left. I just stood there praying and looking at the lady pinned in the driver's seat.

"I'm not sure how long I was there, but I thought I saw a slight flicker through the window. I lifted the police tape, ran to her car, put my hand on her shoulder, and shouted, "Talk to me! Talk to me!" Her eyes opened briefly, and she spoke this number, your phone number. I spoke to the police and then called the number she gave me. They sent the trauma unit from MUSC. I watched and continued to pray and wondered about her chances of living. Then towards the end of the day I received your phone call. I began to rejoice and give thanks to my God."

The beauty and wonder of it all is we still had our daughter, Bobby had his wife, Rosalyn had her mother, and CoraRose had her grandmother.

CHAPTER TWENTY-SEVEN

LIFE IN THE VILLAGE

Rose and I at our "forever home"

The last year and a half have been emotionally, physically, and spiritually challenging. In May 2018 Rose and I said goodbye to our home of fifty years—5813 Lakeview Drive, Hanahan, South Carolina. We moved to our forever home, The Village of Summerville. We have many friends we met while I was working at the Presbyterian Home, as well as people we went to high school with, served with in Vietnam, from Park Circle Presbyterian, and new acquaintances. It is like living in a close community where everyone supports and cares for each other. The Village offers many programs, and I have participated in several, including water aerobics and balance classes. We attend

Me 4 wheeling with my best friends.

concerts, movies, and more. Rose delivers cinnamon buns to every new resident. I continue to take Wendy to see people in the rehab center and memory care. The highlight of my day is driving my golf cart back on a path through the woods, around the ponds and fields, as my little dog runs beside me and explores.

Being at The Village is like being a rich immigrant—the only difference between us and immigrants in the Middle East is we are on a good boat, have a good crew and a good captain. We don't know where we will land but wherever we land will be a good place. My favorite song, which I sing in the shower everyday, is "*Que Sera Sera*, Whatever will be will be, The future's not ours to see, *Que Sera Sera*."

In 2017 I was diagnosed with a rare form of leukemia associated with rheumatoid arthritis (RA) and then Merkel-cell carcinoma skin cancer. After many trips to the hospital, and an operation to remove the Merkel-cell growth, I started twenty-nine days of radiation. On the eleventh day a severe pain erupted and after many tests and procedures, the doctors could not figure out why. A palliative-care doctor stepped into my life and began teaching me ways to self-heal and avoid the pain. This included meditation, which I practice daily, acupuncture, and hypnosis, which takes me to a very peaceful, relaxing place in my mind. Dr. John Franklin has had me visualize and I go to the trout stream in the mountains, or sailing in the harbor. After many unsuccessful trips to the VA to help cure my many illnesses I decided to go on Hospice.

CHAPTER TWENTY-EIGHT

CHILDREN, GRANDCHILDREN, GREAT-GRANDCHILDREN

Family Thanksgiving 2018

In reflection, the most enjoyable and meaningful times in my memories were the times spent with my family, individually and together.

When the kids were younger, there were the camping trips from the mountains to the seashore in our old Winnebago. There were the Little League baseball games and high school basketball games with Rusty and Richard. I never missed one.

Then there were many individual times with each member—Rose and our anniversary trips to the Pisgah Inn at the foot of Mount Pisgah. We hiked almost every trail within miles of the inn with our dog Holly. On our last trip Holly, Rose, and I could manage to walk only to the restaurant one hundred yards away.

When Robin was six years old, we went out to dinner at a famous restaurant in Monterey, California, just the two of us, which was the beginning of monthly dinners at a restaurant of her choice, just the two of us, until she met Bobby, her future husband.

When Rusty was nine years old I took him trout fishing in the mountains of North Carolina. We continued these fishing trips each year, sometimes twice a year, in the spring and in the fall, for the next forty-eight years. In the beginning, we slept in a tent in front of an open fire. In later years I talked him into sleeping at a local motel. When we started, I had to hold him by his belt to walk across a stream. When I had to stop fishing, he was holding me by my belt.

When Richard came into the family nine years after Rusty, we took many trips together, some short, some long. My most memorable was when we went to New York City

GRANDS

My Grands

MY Great grandsons — Sullivan and Shephard Boston (Bradley's sons)

and Washington, D.C. I will never forget the time we got lost on the fifty-sixth floor of the World Trade Center and had to be rescued by construction workers. There was also our trip together to San Francisco when we drove down Route 1, along the coast of California, in a convertible sports car, when Richard was older, married, and employed. It was a Father's Day gift.

My individual times with the kids did not stop when they grew up and left home. The grandkids soon followed.

The first was Rosalyn. She took the place of her mom for our monthly dinner dates. We started off at Applebee's and ended up at a mom-and-pop bookstore when she was at a pre-kindergarten age. As she got older, she would pick more sophisticated restaurants, her favorite being California Dreaming. Since her mother had to be at school early as a teacher I got to eat breakfast with Rosalyn most mornings and then take her to school to the tune of "The Rain in Spain" from the musical *My Fair Lady*.

Then came Bradley, Rusty and Peggy's son. I didn't get to see Bradley as much as I would have liked because he lived with his other grandparents. But when he was five or

My Great granddaughter CoraRose Greene

six he became one of Hanahan's outstanding Little League baseball players. In his first five years I never missed a ballgame. There was one special trip that I had with Bradley when he was nine years old. We spent the day on Hilton Head Island attending a PGA golf tournament. Bradley was able to get an autograph from Tiger Woods.

Eleven years later my miracle granddaughter Emily, daughter of Rusty and Jackie, was born with a defective heart. The first month of her life was spent in the prenatal unit at the Medical University of South Carolina with tubes tied to every part of her body. Someone in the family was at her bedside lovingly rubbing her head until she fell asleep. After three heart surgeries over the first three years of her young life she became a healthy young lady.

Then two years later Emily's sister Katherine was born and became a computer guru before she was six years old.

Six years later Raylynn, the daughter of Richard and Teresa, was born in Atlanta, to be followed two years later by Anna Rose. Because of the distance between Hanahan and Atlanta I didn't get to see Anna and Raylynn as much as the other grandkids, but we made the most of the holidays and frequent visits to Atlanta.

While I've been working on these memoirs there came into my life three beautiful and healthy great-grandchildren. The first was Sullivan, the son of Bradley and Chelsea, followed by CoraRose, the daughter of Rosalyn and J.C., and Shepard, the brother of Sullivan. I had the privilege of being present at the hospital when all my grandchildren and great-grandchildren were born.

I cannot close my story without mentioning my other children—Reeney, Penny, Ginger, and Holly—that brought me unconditional love, joy, and peace of mind. They're now waiting to greet me on the other side of the Rainbow Bridge, tails wagging excitedly. Wendy is still with me and I will be waiting for her on the other side of the bridge.

CHAPTER TWENTY-NINE

LIFE ON HOSPICE
By Robin Boston

My Hospice Angels

As Dad explained, he had rheumatoid arthritis, which is an autoimmune disease, a rare form of leukemia, and Merkel-cell skin cancer that attacks the body with low immunity. After they operated to remove the Merkle-cell growth in his calf (they didn't get it all) he started a twenty-nine-day series of radiation. He rode the VA van from Summerville downtown to the VA each day. He seemed to enjoy the long journey as he met and conversed with fellow veterans. The eleventh day was October 12, 2018, Dad's eighty-fifth birthday. We had planned several celebrations, but we ended up having to take balloons to the VA hospital. It was different this time. We had rushed to the emergency room more than four times in the past year with Dad in excruciating pain. Each time we thought this was the end. But each time, they pumped him with antibiotics and his "magic drug," prednisone, and he was fine for a while. But the "flare-ups," as he called them, started coming closer and closer. He learned to enjoy the good times between, but eventually there came a time when his pain was everywhere, and the doctors couldn't figure out what was wrong or what to do.

Teams of doctors and their students met to set up an interdisciplinary treatment plan. His team of doctors and specialists included: a primary care physician, rheumatologist, oncologist, hematologist, infectious-disease doctor, prosthetist, dermatologist, cardiologist, pulmonologist, surgeons, an anesthesia pain team, acupuncturist, ophthalmologist, occupational therapist, speech doctors, his beloved palliative doctor John Franklin, and nurse Carol Larson. Everyone circled around him, brainstorming to find a solution to ease the pain and keep him alive. Through meditation and hypnosis, Dr. Franklin took him to his happy place on the stream. Dr. Franklin also reminded him that his future and his care was his decision. He kept telling Dad, "Robert, you can decide what you want to do—more MRIs? X-rays? Radiation? Surgery? Or are you ready to stop and be comfortable?" I was beside him as he considered his future of treatment and his options for care. I told him it was okay to let go. Both of us were crying, when he said he didn't want to leave Mom or me. I reassured him we would be okay, and I would take care of Mom and their dog Wendy. He said he would go on Hospice and never wanted to be admitted to the VA hospital again—it was relief.

I remember asking Dr. Franklin how long he thought Dad had to live, knowing this was a hypothetical question. In response, he drew a chart. He said, "Those who stay active will all of a sudden fall off the cliff one day, and those who don't will linger, not in a good way." So, we took Dad home on a high dose of prednisone to prepare for the end.

Lutheran Hospice moved in and brought him a hospital

bed, provided all the numbers to call when any pain set in, oxygen tanks, a wheelchair, and an angel in the form of a nurse, Karen Hodge. Karen became close to our family. She knew him like a book and we could call her day or night if anything went wrong. She came once a week to take his vitals. Sometimes we saw her twice a week when things weren't perfect. Karen sorted his many medications, bandaged his sores, and kept him totally comfortable.

Dad continued being active, exercising, riding his golf cart here and there, visiting the rehab center at the Presbyterian Village and others with Wendy. Despite his efforts to remain busy, he fell victim to a "gloom and doom" attitude for a while, lamenting, "This is the last Christmas," last this, last that. He often repeated, "I'm ready to go," and would ask "Why am I still here?" I sprayed him with my positive energy spray, an essential oil mix of lavender, lemon, and vanilla, and reminded him of his mantra, "Live in the Moment." I wanted him to *live*, not talk about dying; it made people uncomfortable and sad.

So he did begin to live in the moment, and his demeanor and personality took an upswing. A smile was back on his face. We did things together, like when we took the golf cart down a new path and got stuck in the mud. He was mad. We laughed and called the Village security guard to get us out of our misadventure. He began to "preach" to me. He'd tell me, "You know, heaven is right here and now on earth." He'd say, "I think I have one foot in heaven— it's peaceful."

The illness never left him, and it would be wrong to say that his life became perfect, but when something went wrong, when he had another flare-up of pain, his Hospice nurse Karen made it so he was comfortable and felt fine again. Dad continued to see Dr. Franklin, his palliative-care doctor, at the VA hospital and by video conference.

Sometimes Dad looked so good, Dr. Franklin said he didn't need to be on Hospice—he might have two to five years. We nicknamed him "Comeback Bobby." Most days you wouldn't know he was dying. Dr. Franklin would say, "It's not about the numbers, but how you feel. Do what you want to do." And he did. He enjoyed his kids, his grandkids, and his great-grandkids. He spent time outdoors, enjoyed happy hours, visited with friends, went to eat with his lunch buddies, talked on the phone, and reminisced over old photos. When we tried to keep a sniffly grandchild from him for fear he'd get a cold, he'd say it was okay if one of his grandkids took him out—he was ready!

When walking distances became difficult, the VA secured Dad a fancy electric wheelchair. This gave him some freedom and independence. When his hearing became troublesome, the VA provided BlueTooth hearing aids. Though he only got to experience these for one day, he said he could hear in three dimensions!

In the last years, while he was living, he was also practicing dying. He diligently studied death and heaven. Mom said he spent hours alone in his room reading and meditating. He said he was studying to become a mystic. When Dad told me he was studying heaven and practicing to become a mystic, I asked, "How are you doing that?" He really never answered. Perhaps the path to mysticism is as mysterious as heaven itself. If he had finished his chapter on becoming a mystic he might have said how important it is to wonder, to ask questions, to seek.

One person who helped him with his studies was Barbara, a friend and former colleague in counseling who lived at The Village. Barbara, who is a medium, spoke with Dad often about heaven. She had been in contact with Dad's mother, and knew all about her. I talked to Barbara myself about 3 months after Dad's death and asked her questions about her time working with him. She called me back a couple of hours after we spoke, and told me he was there with her. She said he looked wonderful, happy with a smile, and she could hear him "chuckle." She told me she had no idea what sparked his visit, but that maybe it was inspired by my contact with her.

Dad meditated silently and studied books on death and dying. He also searched for answers in the Bible and from scholars of the Bible. Dad, a scholar of the bible himself, followed and read meditations by Richard Rohr daily.

Richard Rohr had a term for this time of transition that Dad found himself in. He called it *liminal space.*

Richard Rohr writes:

> "Liminal spaces enable us to see beyond our-selves to the broader and more inclusive world that lies before us. When we embrace liminality, we choose hope over denial, or despair. The world around us becomes again an enchanted universe… In the unknown space between here and there, younger and older, past and future, life happens. And, if we attend, we can feel the Holy Spirit mov-ing with us in a way that we may not be aware of in more settled times."

This term and the writings of Richard Rohr helped me bet-ter understand the space, the spiritual journey, the place of transformation that Dad was going through. I was an observer of this time and space.

Dad also carried a prayer by Allen Holt, an Episcopal priest, in his wallet all the time.

The prayer says:

"Dear Lord, I wonder, as I get older and have more things go wrong with my body and my mind, what lies ahead. I accept the fact that I have to lay down this life before I can begin another. But I'm still a little bit scared. I like it here. I love my family and my friends. I enjoy living. I like the daily surprises. I even like complaining! I want to live.

"So whether I continue on in this life a while longer or whether I begin my new life sooner than I bargained for, I guess it makes little difference, especially when I realize that as one life ends, another life will begin. As my family and friends cry, 'There he goes,' other family and friends I haven't seen for awhile will be shouting, 'Here he comes!'

"Lord, I place myself in your hands. Please ease my doubts. Deepen my faith. Calm my fears. Touch my aches and pains. Hang on to me and restore my sight. There is a God. And there is more out there than meets the eye. There is a tomorrow. And I'm certain I'll be in it. Amen."

He shared the prayer with lots of people.

Like so many of his other life experiences, Dad used his own time of dying as a time of teaching and learning. He leaned on the experience and the teachings of others to help ready himself, and in turn, his experience inspired me and others in his life to look at death, dying, and heaven in new ways and to find new understandings of the unknown journey ahead of us all whether on this earth or in another life.

The following are memories, poems, excerpts, testimonies, and writings inspired by Bob Boston and his life written by those who loved him.

FOR PAPA
A poem by Rosalyn Cowart Greene

I only have the things they tell me
to know him then.
The oldest son
to a mother not unlike mine,
with a house full
of saved things,
baby dolls,
and tampered family photos.
The son to a father
I never knew
but in the brown pictures
where he stands in front yards,
sits in big chairs.

The chaplain
who wrote letters
flew in planes
held scared hands
and brought home the dolls
with black hair and small eyes
and tiny silk shoes.
I'd like to ask him
Who taught you how to love?

I loved his closet
when I was small enough
to sit between the blazers
that smelled like him
and wooden floors.
I'd twist the tops
off the shoe polishes
he kept in the very back,
fingers black
and brown.
Most mornings
he'd let me pick out
his tie for work,
and my favorite was full of faces,
children in different shades
of white and brown
with eyes
in sizes I'd never seen.

He'd take me to dinner downtown
in my new dress
or new shoes
and once I got my head stuck
between two black bars,
getting as close as I could

to watch some fiddler crabs
below the docks
of the Waterfront Park.
He called me
rising from the bench
where he was watching
me, boats, families.
I tried to pull my head free
firmly –
but nothing.
Again I pulled,
frantic –
rocking and twisting and pulling
rust and tears dripping.
When it was over
and my head was free
he rocked my tired self
until sobs became gasps,
creaks of a wooden swing,
until the only sound left
was a lullaby about the moon
his voice trying,
willing me to peace.

We'd walk the docks
of the marina,
wet wood,
buoys clanking,
sails rolled,
reading the names
off the backs of boats
until we got to the one
that we used to ride
and he'd remember
the harbor

the family laughing
their koozie necklaces
fireworks
and my tiny red lifejacket.

He has a collection
of books on God
that smell like
I think God might smell,
old, wise,
like dust
and familiar hands.

I could sit
in the Chapter Two Bookstore
for hours
in little chairs
listening to him read
about dogs,
about friends,
little girls
and boys
growing up to be
whatever they want to be
as if it were as easy
as turning the page
and changing costumes.

I only have the things they tell me
to know him then,
but this man is the only man
I've ever known,
this giver
shaking hands
in the hall

outside the sanctuary,
his ties, boats,
books, songs, peaces,
and I'd like to ask him
How is it giving everything you have
a second time around?

BOBBY BOSTON: NO ORDINARY PRIEST
By Mitch Carnell

My friend's reality transitioned today.
Our hearts grieve that he could not stay.
Bobby lived life in the present, minute by minute.
"Life is made of what you put in it."
He accepted his condition never afraid.
The natural progression of all things made.
He loved life and lived it to the brim.
His cup ran over bubbling as a hymn.
He sang of dogs, birds and trees
Often while thankful on his knees.
He welcomed young and old.
He brought misfits in from the cold.

He showed all respect, known and unknown
And assured each, "You've found a home."
He was no ordinary priest, no caricature.
He found an anchor that held him secure
Our lives are richer because he was here.
His faith taught us we have nothing to fear.

A Genius for Friendship
By Bert Keller

Bob Boston was one of the people who made me feel
at home in Charleston. He was one of my first friends
in the city when I moved to town in 1969. He and Rose
had been in Charleston a little more than a year. I must
have sensed then that Bob's high art was friendship. He
had a genius for friendship. Ranging from his intimate
relationships to casual meetings in a line at the grocery
store, Bob had the ability to establish and sustain a sense
of "I-thou," a personal connection that, when you experience it, you know that's what life is really about. What a
gift, that sense of calm, unhurried, warm, and open presence that inspires you to be alive and real because he was
always real. I could not have known all that about Bob
when we started hanging out in 1969, but in the span of
fifty years, through kaleidoscopic changes, I found Bob's
friendship deepening yet remaining true to that essence:
calm, warm, open, and inviting presence.

There is a correlation between the gift of friendship and
the gift of healing in a professional counseling relationship. Bob's career in chaplaincy—both military and senior community—and in marriage and family counseling
was stamped with his personal gift of disarming friendship. People warmed to Bob quickly, released their fears,
and became more open and trusting with their partners.

Under the gaze of this caring person they got a stabilizing sense of who they were, and the courage to grow into
that unique and valued person. I don't think his secret
was mastery of a technique: I think his secret was his
own authenticity as a loving, caring human being.

Bob was pastor of Circular Church when I met him. He
was doing things I admired and wanted to be part of.
That was an epoch of great social unrest, the late 1960s
and early '70s. The congregation was small and that allowed Bob to develop a wider, diverse ministry in the
community. Charleston was a haven for hippies and
homeless teenagers and young adults, many living rough
in communes scattered around the city. Bob, backed by
members of Circular, was the only "establishment" adult
I knew of who had a trusting relationship with them, and
in many cases with the parents of young people who had
fled from home. Those were risky and exciting times,
described by Bob in this memoir. Experiences then led directly into his starting, with dear friend Kaye Sharpe, the
first marriage-and-family counseling center in the city,
working still in the context of Circular Church.

Bob had already become a mentor to me when he began
inviting me to share his ministry. Though only about five
years older than me, Bob had a gravity from his experience in Vietnam, and a style of ministry with the Circular
congregation, that commanded my respect and coaxed
me into a more mature ministry of my own. Likewise,
Bob's marriage to Rose and his parenting of Robin, Rusty,
and Richard (who he invited me to baptize at Circular)
were exemplary. He loved and lived passionately with
his family, keeping the bonds fresh and fun and flexible.
When we became colleagues in ministry at Circular, our
different styles and personalities complemented each other, I think, and my respect for him as a mentor increased
through collaboration.

Bob thrived on opportunities to work with troubled teenagers, couples, and small groups, but he was famous for devising ways to avoid preaching sermons. On more than a few Sundays he asked the congregation to write a question on an index card. These were collected and Bob read the questions and improvised answers on the spot, for about twenty minutes. Bob was no egghead and his answers were always pastoral. He was the master of the light touch.

On at least two occasions he had everybody go outside for a "trust walk," one of the trust- building exercises popular in the sensitivity training movement of that time. Pairing off, one person was blindfolded and the other could not speak, and in turns the dumb led the blind for a walk through the somewhat-treacherous graveyard. One very proper lady attended on the first Sunday Bob did that and was so put off by it that she didn't come back for one whole year. She showed up again the very Sunday Bob felt it was time to do it a second time. She was not seen again! Circular was not for everybody, but others found these un-conventionalities a breath of fresh air and the congregation grew with unconventional people. That is, with *real* people.

About a year before he died Bob called me one evening. He had checked into the VA Hospital that morning for cancer surgery, knowing it was a very serious, high-risk operation. He was in surgery for about two hours, and it was successful beyond the surgeon's expectations. "I was sitting in the waiting room at 8:15 and picked up the paper," he said on the phone. "There was your article! I read it and it was written just for me—it was like you were here in the room talking to me and saying the right things. I knew I had to call tonight and let you know that."

I thanked my friend sincerely and warmly. But my thinking was, Bob, you are an artist of affinities! You are such a great soul that you're responsive even to something like that, at a time like that, and you find nourishment to grow, and you use the moment to deepen and enrich a friendship! A few months later, in his Summerville home, Bob said, "I can't recall names, but I SEE the person, the image of their face, and you know where? *Here*," he said, pointing to his heart. That's Bob for as long as I've known him.

Speaking of heart, I think of Bob when I read a passage from Jack Kornfeld's wise book, *A Path with Heart*. Here it is, a toast to Bob:

"The things that matter most in our lives are not fantastic or grand. They are moments when we touch one another, when we are there in the most attentive or caring way. This simple and profound intimacy is the love that we all long for. These moments of touching and being touched can become the foundation for a path with heart, and they take place in the most immediate and direct way. Mother Teresa put it like this: 'In this life we cannot do great things. We can only do small things with great love.'

"In the stress and complexity of our lives, we may forget our deepest intentions. But when people come to the end of their life and look back, the questions that they most often ask are not usually, 'How much is in my bank account?' or 'How many books did I write?' or 'What did I build?' or the like. If you have the privilege of being with a person who is aware at the time of his or her death, you find the questions such a person asks are very simple: 'Did I love well?' 'Did I live fully?' 'Did I learn to let go?'"

Yes, Bob, you certainly did.

Lessons from Papa on Finding Comfort in the Unknown

By Rosalyn Cowart Greene

Corinthians 4:16-18

So we do not lose heart. Even though our outer nature is wasting away, our inner nature is being renewed day by day. For this slight momentary affliction is preparing us for an eternal weight of glory beyond all measure, because we look not at what can be seen; for what can be seen is temporary, but what cannot be seen is eternal.

We sat in the front yard together on the old Charleston bench looking into the blue-black night, my small head in his lap, our voices drifting toward the sky.

> "I see the moon.
> The moon sees me.
> The moon sees the one
> that I want to see.
> "God bless the moon
> and God bless me.
> God bless the one
> that I want to see."

This song would become our song, the song Papa sang to all of his grandchildren, a lullaby I would pass to my own child. We didn't know it then, but these moments of wonder became seeds of comfort, bringing a celestial heaven here to earth.

Years later, in the dark, I held a sleeping baby, her soft cheek warm and wet on my chest, and I sang, our song becoming a prayer. These moments that span decades, were threaded together by a shared love, a shared song, and a message of trusting what is to come, "… because we look not at what can be seen; for what can be seen is temporary, but what cannot be seen is eternal."

John 20: 28

> *Blessed are those who have not seen and yet have come to believe.*

In my last letter to Papa, I wrote about doubt, citing the scripture and Jesus's message to Thomas. I thanked Pa for encouraging me to question in order to define and strengthen my faith. He always emboldened my curiosity and helped me embrace the complexity of doubt. As I had done so many times before sitting beside him, I turned to Papa for wisdom in the letter, not necessarily answers to questions, but guidance, permission to question. I wrote to him about finding contentment in the unknown. If I'm honest, it was as much a message to comfort him as it was an acknowledgement to myself that our time together in this life was dwindling.

It feels odd, I wrote, that one must find more comfort in the unknown than the known, but I like to think that Jesus found more comfort in the complexities of this world than in the certainties. Nothing is certain except the inevitability of change and fluidity and transience. Although permanence seems better to many, impermanence is much more reassuring to me because it means there is always more to behold, more to know, and more to love. This is precisely what Pa taught me in life, to live in the here and now, and look forward to the love to come.

MEMORIES OF BOB/BOBBY BOSTON
BY ROSE McCULLOUGH ERWIN BOSTON

I have loved Bobby since the ninth grade, although he didn't know it. He had lots of girlfriends who swooned over his blue eyes. We got together the summer before our junior year at Furman University, when he decided to go into the ministry and transferred schools. We married June 22, 1956, after graduation, and then went on to seminary and a life full of new places and new friends.

Memories! Lots of good ones and some not so good, but we lasted almost sixty-four years. After each date, we joined little fingers and said, "Through good days, through bad days, forever and always, I love you." Our legacy is our family: three children, four spouses, six grandchildren, three great-grandchildren, six dogs, and two cats. As the poet Mary Oliver wrote: "To live in this world you must do three things: to love what is mortal;

to hold it against your bones knowing your own life depends on it; and, when the time comes to let it go, let it go."

I do miss his presence. He was my one and only love.

Memories by Ronald Eugene Boston

As I share several of my memories of events with my brother Bobby, and the immense influence he had on my life, I would point out that to share all of my memories would necessitate writing my own memoir. I will later share the three most significant and impactful memory events that in large measure determined the path of my life.

From the age of about five to eight, when Bobby was about nine to twelve, he served many times as a surrogate parent and/or babysitter to my sister Joy and me. He was "the man of the house" when Mother and Dad were away. To care for a girl aged two to five and a rambunctious five-to-eight year-old boy was an awesome responsibility to place on a boy his age. However, he handled those chores well, as evidenced by his and our survivals.

My very first memory in this life is the story Bobby

relates about locking me in our living room behind window-paned double doors one winter night when I acted out as a five year old. Its significance here is only that it is my very first memory, and here, I surmise, is the reason: The living room, in addition to having no heat, was also very dark, and Bobby was "booing" at me like a "boogie man" and sticking out his tongue with his face against a glass pane at about my height. I am sure it is my first memory because of my stark fear of the cold and dark room and my anger at being locked there. Bobby has proof that I busted through the pane with my left fist by a scar above his left eyebrow. Well, I also have proof of that event by an eighty-one year-old scar on the inside of my left forearm.

After we moved to Spring Street in Darlington in 1943, Bobby and I always shared the upstairs bedroom and we were bedmates until he left for Wofford in the fall of 1952. I had attended most, if not all, of my brother's high school football and basketball home games and many of his tennis matches. In short, from my age of about nine to eighteen, Bobby was my hero and role model. In other words, through my high school days, my work and sport endeavors almost literally followed his example and in his footsteps. From time to time, as my brother traveled down his river of life to the sea of the hereafter, his sage advice and inspirations played a very large role in my own travels.

This brings me to the three significant memory events that shaped my life. The first was Bobby's Christmas gift to me in 1955, his senior year at Furman University and my junior year of high school. It was a leather-bound King James version of the Bible with a personal and inspirational message written on the inside cover. I read this Bible, generally, in our bedroom at night and at other times or occasions when confronted with some stress or unhappiness in my high school life. Thereafter, I used it in my required religious classes during my two years at Presbyterian College. Although somewhat worn and taped together in places, the Bible remains on a bookshelf in my home office today.

A second, and perhaps the most significant and impactful memory event, is my visit over the Thanksgiving weekend in 1956, to the one-room apartment of Bobby and Rose in Atlanta, Georgia. It was Bobby's first year at the seminary. I believe they came to Darlington for Thanksgiving day, and I returned with them to Atlanta, as Rose had to work on Friday. I slept on the sofa in the living room. Bobby gave me a tour on Friday of the seminary and part of Atlanta. We all went ice skating that evening, a first for me. On Saturday, we attended the Georgia vs. Georgia Tech football game, and grilled out at the apartment that night. On Sunday we traveled to Bobby's Wayside Presbyterian Church where I heard him preach for the first time. Boy, was I impressed! After the service we had a picnic lunch at the church and visited with his congregation. We returned to Atlanta that evening. Monday morning I said my goodbyes to Bobby and Rose and proceeded to thumb rides back to Darlington (it was safe in that day and time).

It was during this visit that my brother asked me about my plans for the future after graduation the next spring. Unlike Bobby, who had dated a lot of girls during high school, I had dated one girl and we were talking marriage. I told Bobby that I planned to join the navy, marry her when she graduated in 1958, and, after a four-year tour, maybe go to college on the GI Bill or get a job. He replied to the effect that it would be a better plan to delay marriage and the military, work hard next spring and summer, save my money, and apply to a college, perhaps his first college, Wofford. He even said that he and Rose could probably help me with some of my finances if necessary. This was his sage advice and the inspiration that propelled my life's objectives from that moment forward. It led to a BA degree in Economics at USC in 1961, followed by a Doctor of Laws degree in 1965. I practiced law in Columbia for forty-four years with the same law firm that I clerked for in law school. I began as the fifth attorney in a five-attorney firm and retired in 2007 as the senior partner in a ninety-five-attorney firm with offices in five South Carolina cities. I want it understood that I relate this history not to promote any of my own accomplishments, but only to punctuate this memory event and the cherished example of my brother's wise advice in Atlanta in 1956. I have so far lived a very happy and fairly successful life on my journey down the river, and it is with much love and a monumental tribute to and gratitude for my brother.

Finally, when I was about seventy-five and Bobby was eighty-one and his maladies were increasing, he and I engaged in a number of conversations, primarily by phone, about life and confronting and traversing its end to the hereafter. Once again his wisdom and, this time, his learned teachings came to the front. My brother introduced me to two books and a prayer about the journey through this life and dealing with the end-of-life issues that we all must face at some point with faith and courage and with as much grace as we can. The books are *Being Mortal* by Atul Gawande and *When Breath Becomes Air* by Paul Kalanithi. The prayer he sent to me on, I believe, on my seventy-fifth birthday, I have tucked into my top dresser drawer. Periodically, I retrieve it and read it over again for the comfort it gives me. I have also photographed it on my cell phone and computer, and I share it with some of my friends and golfing buddies. I have also included it in cards to a number of friends who are ill and going through end-of-life issues, trusting it gives them the comfort it gives me. For these books and the prayer I again pay tribute to and give thanks and love to my brother.

To my brother, Bobby, I say goodbye for now. Even in your death and the end of your journey through this life to the next, you have again rendered help to me as I continue down my river of life. I am further comforted by the thought that one day, and not too far off, comparatively speaking, I will be reunited with you and others of our loved ones.

MEMORIES BY PEGGY JOY BOSTON BURNEY

As my father was a traveling salesman, he was rarely home when I was a little girl. My big brother Bobby was my stand-in dad. He was so loving and was always there for me when I cried. My mother used to tell me I was rotten because neither Bobby nor my dad would let me cry or want for anything. She said Bobby held me way too much and loved giving me my bottle.

When Dad left on Mondays, he told Bobby, "Help your mom all you can and make Ronnie and Joy behave. You are the man of the house when I'm gone." Then he kissed us all good bye. As long as I had Bobby, I felt everything would be fine.

When I was born, Ronnie, my other brother, was three

years old and Bobby was eight. Ronnie was my favorite playmate. He and I really gave Bobby a lot of trouble. I must have been two or three when we moved from an apartment to our home on Spring Street and Bobby had a big bicycle. He put me in the basket and Ronnie on the back and we rode all over our little town of Darlington. He was my hero. When Ronnie would act up—which he did often—Bobby spanked him or tried to correct him and I cried. Ronnie was my best friend. He played with me and my toys. The three of us stayed best buddies for always. Bobby was our protector.

When we moved, Bobby, because he was the oldest, got the pick of the bedrooms. He chose the upstairs, which was the best room in the house, with two windows on the front looking over the trees and neighborhood. I felt like a bird looking out those windows. We all wanted that room, but it was totally off limits to Ronnie and me. We tried sneaking up there whenever we could. Mother said Bobby took us up occasionally for minutes. But when I acted out at bedtime he took me upstairs and sang to me and told me stories about me as a baby. I did love him so much.

MEMORIES BY ROBIN LYNN BOSTON

June 9, 1984

Robin is the feminine of Robert. Dad was my spiritual advisor. He was the first man in my life; we had a close bond, as he did individually with all of his children. Since I was a little girl we went on dates to fancy restaurants—just the two of us. He taught me so much about life! He pounded things into me, like: Everyone is unique, and you should never try to change someone—let them be themselves; Never judge, live in the moment.

When my old cars broke down and I prayed about it, he said God had more important things to deal with than your Toyota—have you been tithing? He taught me the importance of giving and I have never stopped. "You are only poor in Spirit" — this came from his mom, my Granny. "Live in the moment, heaven is here on Earth."

He was full of adventure, and gave me my sense of adventure and exploration. He taught me to swim, he taught all his children and grandchildren to drive, he bought a sailboat, Winnebago, motorcycle, and convertible and went on road trips with his friends. We camped, we kayaked and rafted, we sailed, we waterskied and snow skied, we traveled to New York, and recently to Spain, San Francisco, Boston. We climbed rocks on Pebble Beach and searched for golf balls, we saw the Grand Canyon, redwood forests....

He LOVED animals—he fed the squirrels, his fish, the birds, and he had a spiritual bond with dogs. We always had dogs and cats. Once I found some abandoned baby squirrels and we raised them until we let them go, but they never left. He swears the squirrels that were in his yard the day he moved were their descendants. He wanted to take them with him to The Village. (I think they moved to my yard, so I feed them.) No wonder his favorite Bible verse is about the animals. He trained them as therapy dogs and reading dogs and volunteered at hospitals, schools, even took his dog to calm college students during exam week.

Everywhere we went someone knew him. Even when he wasn't there, and I would tell someone my name, they asked me if I was kin to Bob Boston. People remembered his piercing blue eyes, and he *always* looked you in the eyes. He had a calming way, he was a great listener. He said *everyone* is beautiful and you could see the beauty if you look in their eyes.

He was very protective of me. When I went home alone, he came in my house and checked the closets to make sure no one was there. He got mad when I didn't lock my doors, so he bought me a push-button lock.

About two years ago, he invited me to his weekly luncheon with some of his best friends, mostly retired ministers, medical professionals, all elderly, wise men who shared his same views. They invited me to become part of their group, said they needed a feminine perspective, but I know he wanted me to have them be my father-like advisors.

Since I am holistic, I always gave him the latest natural cures (I'm sometimes called a witch doctor) and he half-heartedly took them. I had him on Frankincense, apple cider vinegar and essential oils, high-Ph water, and other questionable cures. He always said we were trying to keep him alive but when God said it was time, who do you think is going to win? I think we were the winners to have him around so long. He got wiser and wiser and I spent every minute I could with him. We spent every Tuesday together going to lunch, riding around on the golf cart, and talking about big things, Life.

One of my fondest memories of Dad was the song he sang to all his children, grandchildren, and great-grandchildren. Whenever I see the moon, I sing it and remember:

> "I see the moon, the moon sees me, the moon sees the one that I want to see. God bless the moon and God bless me and God bless the one that I want to see.
>
> "I believe that God above created you for me to love. He picked you out from all the rest because he knew I'd love you best.
>
> "I love you and you love me. We pledge it now

for all to see. God Bless you and God bless me and God bless all that we want to see.

"God bless the moon and God bless me, together we will always be. And one day soon we'll be as one; if it's God's will, it will be done."

He always told me that God is with you every minute. He is your breath and when you need to get in touch, quiet your mind and breathe, listen, feel, he will be with you. I was with Dad when he took his last breath. I can feel God and Dad's spirit, especially by the mountain stream. I know he is always there for me. I miss him so.

Bob the Builder and Rocking Robin, Juarez 2004

A Letter to Dad
by Russell Erwin Boston

Dear Dad, my best friend,

I cannot begin to write down all the memories we shared together in our journey of life. Our memories are forever embedded in my heart. Your love as a father created my desire to always want to be with you. It was at an early age I knew we were inseparable and that is why you became my best friend.

I remember the countless Saturdays I walked with you on the golf course, learning how to caddie, and the countless times you allowed me to run ahead to the next tee box just to hit a golf ball. It was this that gave me the desire that one day you and I would play golf together. During baseball season, you chipped golf balls in the "right of way" while I caught the balls with my glove. The hours I spent watching you play tennis created the path for you and me to become tennis partners for fifty years. You gave me a passion to love the outdoors with all the camping trips, fly-fishing trips, and hiking trips that we took together. I remember walking the stream banks watching you fly fish and wanting so badly to come into the water with you but knowing it was so cold. You eventually bought me my own waders at a consignment shop, and I didn't mind that they leaked, Dad, as long as I was in the water with you. I remember the countless times you held on to me while we crossed difficult stretches of water just for you to reach that special spot that you promised would hold a rainbow trout. Our lunch breaks by the river were special times. That is where you taught me how to eat cold pork and beans from a can and Vienna sausage on crackers.

It was the transition, Dad, that we both witnessed that proved our powerful love for each other. I began taking you on fly-fishing trips, preparing gourmet meals by the stream and helping you across difficult stretches of water, promising you that there is our trophy trout. We started our fly-fishing adventures when I was six years old. You held me by the belt so I could stand in the stream. Forty-nine years later I held you by the belt so you could stand in the stream. Dad, it was November 2, 2016, when our traditional father-and-son fly-fishing trips came to an end. I dressed you in your waders, tied your boots, prepared your rod and helped you to your favorite spot on the North Mill River. As I walked you out into the stream and held on to you, I noticed you still had the art of casting that fly to that perfect spot and you caught and reeled in your last trout.

I can understand now, Dad, how powerful the love of our progression through life held on to us. I knew you to be always loving and nurturing, to be warm-hearted and soft, and to be caring and thoughtful. There are no words to describe my immense love for you. I wish I would have spent more time with you. All our memories are thickly embedded within my heart. *You will always be alive in my heart.* You were my best friend, Dad. I will miss you dearly! *I love you! Forever.*

MEMORIES BY RICHARD BOSTON

I have spent the last few years trying not to think of the day Dad would leave this world. Atlanta commutes leave a lot of time for reminiscing. A lot of time to reflect on how Dad has impacted me.

Dad was a family man through and through. He and Mom's top priority was instilling in us important family values and they are the reason we have such a close family today.

He taught us that one of the most important gifts you can give your loved ones is your time. We were not a wealthy family, but he went out and bought a Winnebago and toured around the beaches and mountains, spending valuable family time together.

Later he bought a sailboat and we toured the harbor as a bunch of greenhorns. Looking back, we were a danger out there, but it was a means to spend time with family.

I recall one instance, Dad thinking we had the right of way over an oil tanker coming into the harbor because we were under sail. I can still hear the horn blasting at us today. Or running aground out at Capers Island and having to wait half the night for high tide to roll in. But mostly I remember all of us working together, learning how to sail, and letting Mother Nature guide us. Those were good family times. And the value stuck as Teresa and I later used that justification to buy a boat, which we continue to use to strengthen our family bond.

He spent one-on-one time with each of us, Robin, Rusty, and myself. He took week-long trips with us individually. He and Rusty went trout fishing; he traveled to New York City with Robin, where I'm sure he allowed her to drag him through museum after museum while beaming with pride. I remember the trips he and I took to New York City and Washington, D.C., Six Flags, and, more recently, San Francisco. These were invaluable bonding times.

He was a giving person and taught us the joy of helping others. Although I was too young to remember, one story I've been told was when I played T-ball, the coach announced that uniform money was due and if you were late or even couldn't pay, your kid couldn't play. Well, I'm told Dad approached the coach to tell him he would take care of the uniforms for any family that couldn't pay.

I recall one holiday season, we were driving around with a bunch of twenties and he stopped the car and had me get out and give one to people on the street asking for help. That memory still sticks with me today, as sometimes I'll reach in my wallet and give to someone on the streets in need of a helping hand. I will miss his stories and his wherewithal in seeing the good in everyone.

He taught us many life lessons over the years and one of

those was how to be independent.

He wasn't a financial guru by any means, but he taught me the value of a dollar on many occasions. One instance I recall was when I went to Clemson, he gave me a Texaco credit card to put gas in my truck. It didn't take long until he realized that I could buy beer with that card and my buddies and I were partying on his dime. He quickly took it away and reminded me that he paid for necessities and I was on my own for everything else, forcing me to get a job. Raylynn, Anna—Y'all need to be ready one day because I'm definitely passing that policy down to you.

More recently, Dad taught me about the Circle of Life. You start as a child and you end up right back where you started, once again as a child. The closer to the end it came, the more I saw this in him. I was taking care of him the way he at one time took care of me. He taught me about Living in the Now, not worrying about the future or the past, but living in your present moment. As always, he practiced what he preached and lived in the moment, not just from day to day, or even hour to hour, but minute by minute.

One last lesson I learned from Dad was as he was lying there, not far from the end, that his favorite song was "Que Sera, Sera (Whatever Will Be, Will Be)." This has stuck with me since. It's now in my playlist and I will always think of Dad when life gets tough and tough decisions need to be made and I'll say to myself, "Don't worry about it, Whatever Will Be, Will Be."

I could go on for a long while talking about Dad and bragging about the father he was and will continue to be as long as I live.

I'll never be the man Dad was, but his influence will

always be with me. The day he died, I heard Rosalyn tell CoraRose that while PaPa is in heaven, he will always be in her heart. He can now go to school with her or the doctor with her, out to play, or wherever she goes. I believe that is also true with me and for each of us who he has touched, which I venture to say is most of us here today. I can certainly feel his presence here. As time moves on, the tears come less and less because I realize he will always be with me, as I go to work, when I hike or am out on the lake, or wherever my future takes me. He will continue to live in my heart and continue to be the loving father he's always been.

Thanks, Dad. I'll never forget you and I'll love you always.

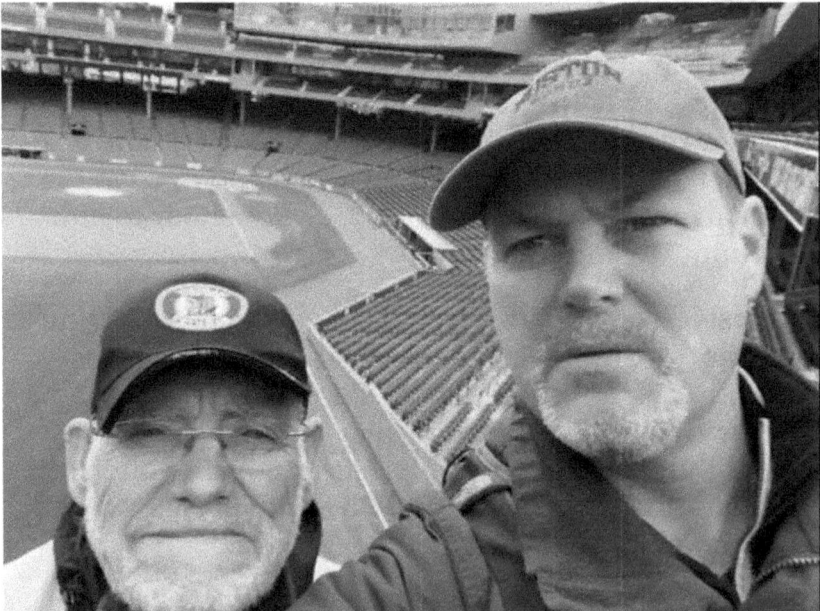

A Eulogy for PaPa
by Rosalyn Cowart Greene

A calm and steady power was his, like a held hand or a full breath. To be in his presence was to feel something special.

As a child, I knew Pa possessed this comforting power, experienced it, had the blessing to be near him almost every day of my life, to swing beside him, to ride on his back, to hold his hand, to watch the sky, the birds, the sails, the ocean, to sing, to spy the moon shining in a deep sea of night. He taught me to see the richness of this earth.

He taught me how to ride the waves of the ocean, holding my small trusting body against the board with his own. "Kick," he would demand, and together we'd kick, anticipating the ocean's strong force, and then the feeling of flying as we rose above the water, on top of the wave, tumbling to shore, laughing.

As I grew up his wisdom revealed itself further. In middle school, he bought me a book on being more assertive. He had me listening to Richard Rohr in college, living in the now, to pull me from the dark spiral of anxiety. I witnessed the way he could calm a storm, beheld how he could help one swim in a strong current. He taught me to respect the power of the current, to see its beauty, to exist with it—not against it, and be set free.

Every morning PaPa drove me to school, waited with me in the car until the first bell rang. We'd sing our favorite songs from the musical *My Fair Lady*, belting out the words to "The Rain in Spain," "I Could Have Danced All Night," and his favorite, "Get Me to the Church on Time."

We'd go on dates every month, just PaPa and me from the time I was about two. Oh, how special I felt! He let me pick the restaurant, usually somewhere in downtown Charleston. Our favorite became California Dreaming, and we'd wait as long as it took for a seat by the window where we could watch the sailboats in the harbor. We'd walk the Waterfront Park, crossing our fingers that a swing would be empty, and usually there was a nice couple who was just getting ready to leave, more than happy to give their swing to a grandfather and his excited little granddaughter. There on that swing, my hand in his, was that feeling of flying again, a comforting memory I would return to often in my life.

And together on the last day PaPa spent in this life, we closed our eyes and we sang, we swam, and we swung.

When I first sat down to write and gather my thoughts to share after Pa left, I wanted so badly to recall the best piece of advice he ever gave, to conjure some conversation over dinner and remember it word for word. I wanted what I now know is impossible, for my time with Pa cannot be summed up with a mantra or even represented by a favorited piece of advice, because it isn't one moment that defines us, it is the gathering of moments that makes our love so rich.

People approached me with comforting scripture after he had gone, and the most popular was John 14:2: "In my Father's house are many mansions…. I go to prepare a place for you." In some translations, "there are many rooms prepared." The more I thought of this, and the more time I spent dwelling in the memories PaPa and I shared, I realized you can't know in a single moment the capacity of love that is being built, but by and by the days go on and a mansion of many rooms reveals itself.

The last chapter of his book on becoming a mystic went unwritten, but anyone who had the pleasure to speak with him about heaven knew he felt heaven was here on earth.

CoraRose, my four-year-old, has a lot of questions about heaven, which I think makes her somewhat of a mystic, too. Where is heaven? How do you take a bath in heaven? Can I go to heaven to visit? Do you have a head in heaven? *Is that heaven*, she asks as we pass a cemetery of stones, bright plastic flowers, scattered plots. *I don't think so*, I answer slowly, and I see a subtle turn in her as she realizes I don't have all of the answers as she expected. One of many of these turns she'll take, we'll take, her and I. And this is when I try to tell her that sometimes it's okay not to know, to only know a little bit. I think PaPa would say it's okay not to know, it's more than okay, it's the true meaning of a mystic—a searcher, a seeker. The questions themselves are the way to Christ and heaven, not the answers. And so, when she asks what happens when we die, I tell her we become love. This is true, I'm certain of it. Because PaPa's love, the mansion of many rooms it built in my life and the lives of others, lives on.

And so I'll leave you with the last lines of a poem by Merritt Malloy that Mammy had printed and tucked in the pages of a worn book.

> "Love doesn't die,
> People do.
> So, when all that's left of me
> Is love,
> Give me away."

MEMORIES BY BRADLEY CHARLES BOSTON

My greatest memory and the best time we had together was when he taught me how to play golf. Me, my dad, and Papa would go to Stono Ferry and play. And when I got older he picked me up from elementary and middle school and took me to the Naval Weapons Station to play. He was always there to listen and offer counseling advice when I was going through a rough time. He

told me, "You have to mess up to learn." It meant a lot to me and my wife Chelsey when he gave us marriage counseling and officiated our wedding.

Memories by Emily Ann Boston

When I decided I was going to speak today I asked my grandma what I should talk about. She asked me if there was a memory or special moment that I shared with him that I could share with others. After a long time of thinking I realized there wasn't. There isn't one special memory I have to share because I don't have just one memory. I have all of them.

I remember him bringing Holly, his therapy dog, to read to my first-grade class. I remember sitting on his lap in a rocking chair on the porch of a beach house while he sang "I see the moon." I remember him driving me to school every morning, coming to watch me cheer at my high school and then college games. He was always there, always a constant. When I get sad and remember that he won't see me become a nurse or get married, I think back to all the things he was a part of and how he is in a better place, doing better than any of us. We will forever love and miss you, Papa.

Memories by Katherine Grace Boston

You can't put into words the memories and lessons that you cherish from someone's life. I know I certainly can't even try to form the words that would describe the influence and relationship I had with my Papa. You would have had to know him to understand the difference that he could make in someone's life. He could make one of your most disappointing days feel like it was the smallest battle. Anytime I struggled in school he would tell me that if I failed he would be even more proud of me because you learn more by failing than by always succeeding.

Not everyone gets to have the relationship with their grandparents that I had. We were together every single day. He taught me so many things, like to be caring and how to love. There's never been a kinder man. He dedicated so much of his time to children and animals; but most importantly to his grandchildren. My sister and I spent every school morning with him. We all joined together with breakfast and he would always request his favorite prayer be said before we ate. It was my kindergarten prayer that he added his own words to so that it could be inclusive to everyone:

> Little hands and little hearts,
> big hands and big hearts,
> bow our heads in prayer,
> thank you, God, for food and drink
> and tender loving care.

He drove us to school singing the whole way and talking to us about what our day would hold. His classical music blared and the dogs always hung their heads out the windows barking at every single kid. As embarrassed as I was, I cherish every one of those moments now. When we were younger, every couple of months he made a point to take us individually out on dates. My favorite spot was California Dreaming. He would get dressed up and we would go to dinner where he would tell me stories of his life and teach me how a real man should treat me when I grew up.

As I got older, we still spent so much time together. He took my sister and me on our first train ride, to Darlington, to show us where he grew up and met Mammy. He showed us our great-grandparents and the houses they lived in as children. I always thought my grandparents would live forever. When they moved during my junior year is when I finally understood they wouldn't be with me forever. I had to go to school by myself and ate breakfast alone for the first time in eight years. I'm forever thankful for everything Papa did for me. He promised me my first car and made sure I got it. I still continue to understand more of the lessons he taught me every day.

MEMORIES BY RAYLYNN BOSTON

Compared to my other family members, who lived only a short drive away, I didn't get to spend a lot of time with PaPa. Our visits were usually limited by things like work or school, but even in those small portions of time, we found time to make memories that I will always remember. I don't necessarily remember exact moments, but I remember the feelings I felt radiate from Pa, such as pride and happiness. Whenever we were at breakfast and someone approached the table, he never hesitated to tell them that he made our beautiful family.

Another memory I have is from one of the visits a week or so before his death. He wanted to fill the bird feeder outside. Even though it was a small task, he was so excited to do it and have me helping by his side. Papa always made sure each and every one of us felt loved. He was a very loving man, spending time visiting at the rehab center, VA, and reading with children. Whenever we went to the farmers' market, he always had Wendy sitting on his walker. When people came by and asked to pet her, he was always patient. Seeing that from afar I felt pride that he was my grandpa. I wanted to tell everyone there that I had the privilege of being related to someone so great. I aspire to live the humble lifestyle that PaPa lived. He lived a fulfilling life from his memories to his friends and family. In the end, my goal is to be as loving, caring, and devoted as my role model, PaPa.

MEMORIES BY ANNA ROSE BOSTON

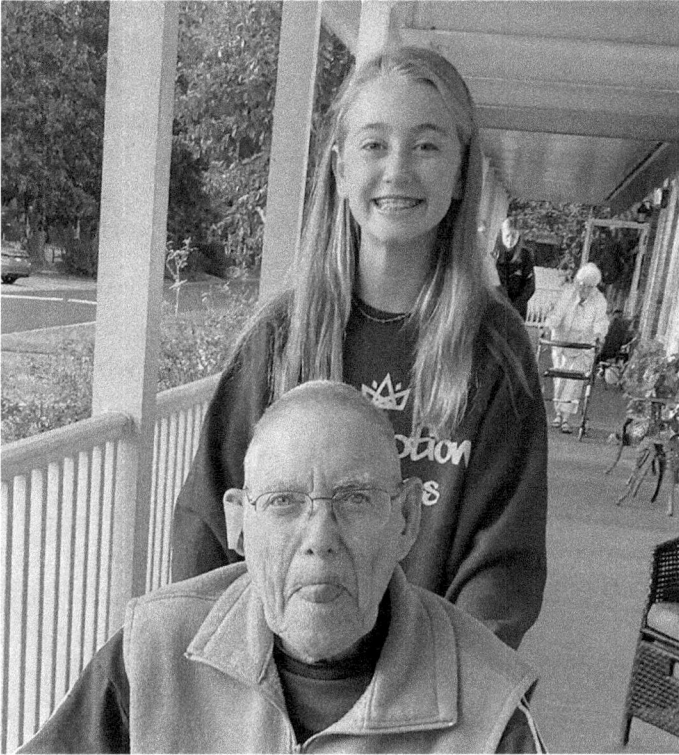

When I was a newborn, Papa held me in his arms and
sang "I See the Moon." As I watched a video of it I have
learned Papa's nature of being a loving grandfather. Papa
taught me and my family valuable lessons as I got to
know him over the years. During his time as a pastor he
preached the most heartwarming sermons. I recall one
time when my dad and I were on our way to Charleston
we listened to one of his sermons about grief. "Never let
grief build up inside you," he explained. "The longer it
sits and builds inside your body the worse it gets." I like
to think that this was a sign on how to deal with his passing. Papa would want us to say that he went to heaven
with his mom and dad and with his dogs.

Papa was the best grandpa a granddaughter could ask for. The times we spent together were short and not frequent, but they were memorable. He could make your day better by smiling at you. He seemed to know the solution to every problem. Papa was so positive and he loved anyone and everyone, no matter where they came from. He taught me to be kind even when I was upset, Papa taught me to be courageous and brave, and, most importantly, Papa taught me to have faith and follow God even during the hardest times.

My Papa is with me everywhere I go. I believe Papa is watching me from heaven. Some of my favorite times I spent with him were on the golf cart. Every afternoon at 5 p.m. he would take his dog Wendy on the golf cart. Sometimes my sister and I would have just gotten to Charleston after being in the car for five hours and he would insist we go on the golf cart. Of course I didn't mind it. Wendy ran behind the golf cart, occasionally stopping for a pee break. Many people knew Papa and knew he lived every day of his life with strength and dignity.

I love my Papa and will always cherish his memory.

Memories by Melissa Joy Burney

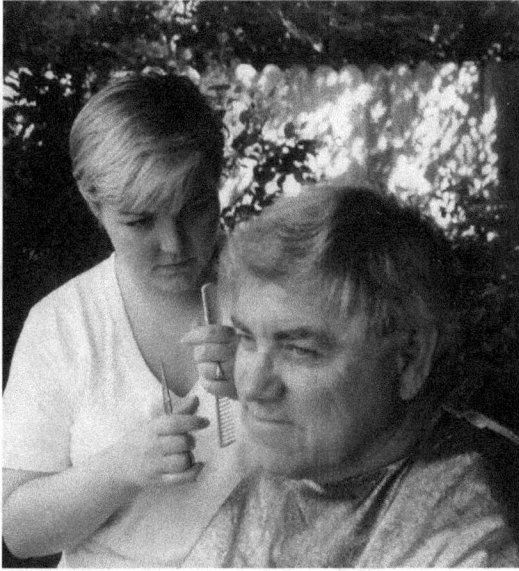

My daughter Halima stated that she didn't feel she knew her great-uncle Bobby very well, and I tried to respond without crying and couldn't. Where my daddy seemed tough, Bobby made me understand it was okay to show feelings. I never heard him raise his voice. Sometimes he came off as almost slow, but it was because he was thinking about the right words to say. He was one of the few who listened instead of waiting to speak. He once spoke of the weeds among the roses. He was both. A rose who could spread love through cracks in concrete if necessary. His faith was a huge and small part of him at the same time. A true Christian without judgment and all were welcomed at his table. And he was ready to converse for hours, to understand your thought process while sharing his. You never felt stupid or wrong after you talked with him, just uplifted. Until he was gone I didn't understand the impact he made on my life. I love and miss you and hope from here forward I can follow more closely in your footsteps.

ROBERT WARNER BOSTON
October 12, 1933 - February 29, 2020

Robert Warner Boston, Summerville –

Robert Warner Boston, 86, husband of Rose Erwin Boston of The Summerville Presbyterian Village, passed to another life on February 29, 2020. Bob was born in Kansas City, Missouri on October 12, 1933 to the late Elmo Edward Boston and Margarita Austin Boston. Bob was raised from the age of 7 in Darlington, SC. He was a graduate of Furman University, Columbia Theological Seminary, and received a Masters Degree in Family Education from Southern Illinois University. He also attended the American Institute for Family Relations in Los Angeles, CA.

While residing in Kansas City, MO, Bob served as the Associate Minister of South Presbyterian Church from 1959-1960 and the minister of Northminster Presbyterian Church from 1960-1965. He served as a Chaplain in the US Army from 1965-1968. His service took him to Vietnam in 1966.

In 1968, Bob became the minister of The Circular Church of the Presbyterian Church USA and the United Church of Christ in Charleston, SC. In 1974, Bob founded the Marriage and Family Counseling Center of Circular Church where, he remained director until 1981. From 1993 to 1998, Bob served as director of the Lutheran Family Counseling Center in Charleston, SC. He was a Chaplain for Lutheran Hospice from 1998 to 2000, when he became the Chaplain for the Presbyterian Village of Summerville, SC where he served until 2005. Bob was an adjunct professor in the Department of Family Practice of the Medical University of South Carolina, the Department of Health and Education of College of Charleston, the Department of Sociology of Charleston Southern University, and at Trident Technical College. He was an approved supervisor for the American Association for Marriage and Family Therapy (AAMFT), past president of the SCAMFT, and member of the Family Mediation Association. Bob was a member of the SC Commission on Alcoholism and the Charleston County Commission on Substance Abuse.

He is survived by his wife Rose of 63 years; one daughter, Robin Boston (Robert Cowart) of Hanahan, SC; sons, Rusty Boston (Jackie) of Goose Creek, SC and Richard Boston (Teresa) of Alpharetta, GA; 6 grandchildren, Rosalyn Cowart Greene (J.C.), Bradley Boston (Chelsey), Emily Boston, Katherine Boston, Raylynn Boston, and Anna Rose Boston; 3 great-grandchildren, Sullivan Boston, CoraRose Greene, and Shepherd Boston, and his beloved dog Wendy. He is also survived by two siblings, Ronnie Boston (Sherrie) of Columbia, SC and Joy Burney (Fred) of Santee, SC.

… In lieu of flowers, Memorial gifts may be sent to The Residents' Assistance Fund c/o Summerville Presbyterian Village, 201 West 9th North Street, Summerville, SC 29483 or the Charleston Animal Society at 2455 Remount Road, North Charleston, SC 29406 (Charlestonanimalsociety.org).

—Charleston *Post and Courier*,
February 29 and March 1, 2020

ACKNOWLEDGEMENTS

I know that if Dad had lived to finish this book, he would have wanted to thank all the loving people who helped put his memoir together. He would thank: Rosalyn for asking the question. Mitch Carnell for pushing and encouraging him to write as well as listening to every word. Rose, Robin, Richard, Rusty and their siblings as well as extended family for finding photos, sharing information, and contributing memories. Robin for typing, and Steve Hoffius for editing and putting it all together, Paul Rossmann for the book design and cover. There is a long list of names on his "In Appreciation "list (over 60). You know who you are if you touched his life or he touched yours.

May you find heaven on Earth.   —RB